CONVERSATIONS WITH the CHILDREN of NOW

CRYSTAL, INDIGO, AND STAR KIDS SPEAK
ABOUT THE WORLD, LIFE, AND THE
COMING 2012 SHIFT

MEG BLACKBURN LOSEY, MSC.D., PH.D.

NEW PAGE BOOKS
A division of The Career Press, Inc.
Franklin Lakes, NJ

CONVERSATIONS WITH THE CHILDREN OF NOW
EDITED BY GINA TALUCCI
TYPESET BY EILEEN DOW MUNSON
Cover design by Scott Fray
Printed in the U.S.A. by Book-mart Press

To order this title, please call toll-free 1-800-CAREER-1 (NJ and Canada: 201-848-0310) to order using VISA or MasterCard, or for further information on books from Career Press.

The Career Press, Inc., 3 Tice Road, PO Box 687,
Franklin Lakes, NJ 07417
www.careerpress.com
www.newpagebooks.com

Library of Congress Cataloging-in-Publication Data
Losey, Meg Blackburn.
    Conversations with the children of now : Crystal, Indigo, Star and
    transitional children speak about the world, life, and the coming
    2012 shift / by Meg Blackburn Losey.
        p. cm.
    Includes index.
    ISBN-13: 978-1-56414-978-7
    ISBN-10: 1-56414-978-1
        1. Children—Psychic ability. 2. Children—Miscellanea.
    3. Parapsychology. I. Title.

BF1045.C45L68 2008
133.8083—dc22

                                                    2007036027

DEDICATION

*T*o humanity,

The possibilities of infinite tomorrows

are within our awakening.

Acknowledgments

Since its inception, this book has been a labor of love. I know that if I try to name every name, and honor every soul who has participated in this work, surely I will miss someone.

To each of the children who have participated with me to bring their words to you, the reader, my love, my heart, and my deepest gratitude for your courage and the wisdom you have brought to these pages. I stand in awe of you.

Each of these wonderful children has a support system, parents, teachers, and others who have participated in the background by writing their answers and their biographies, and gently encouraging the children to be who they are. To each of you I say "Bravo!" and thank you.

To Sunny Ariel for giving me permission to use the interview that we taped with Scotty, I am ever grateful.

Joy Kauf, our meeting in Denver was kismet. The world will be a great place because you took the time to encourage your students and their parents to contribute to this work. Eternal thanks.

To everyone who reads this book, not only do I thank you, but I encourage you to pass it on to your children's teachers, doctors, and anyone else you feel will listen to what the children have said.

Posthumously to my *most* wonderful friend Van Villanti, you remain the greatest example of a supportive friend that my life has ever known. When I get stuck, I still ask that question, "What would Van say?" And still I listen to your wisdom.

To New Page and Career Press, particularly Laurie Kelly-Pye and Michael Pye, thank you for sharing your faith in me and my books with the world.

And to my David, I love how you believe in everything that I do.

CONTENTS

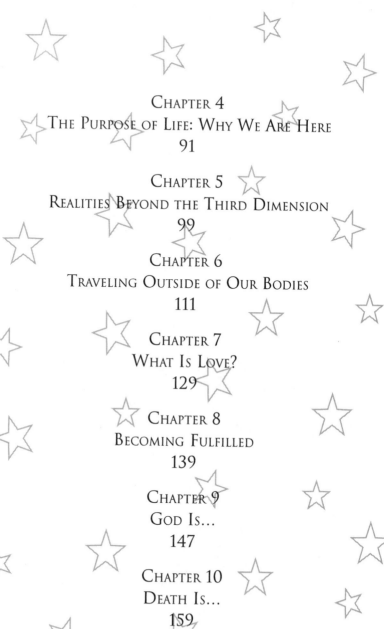

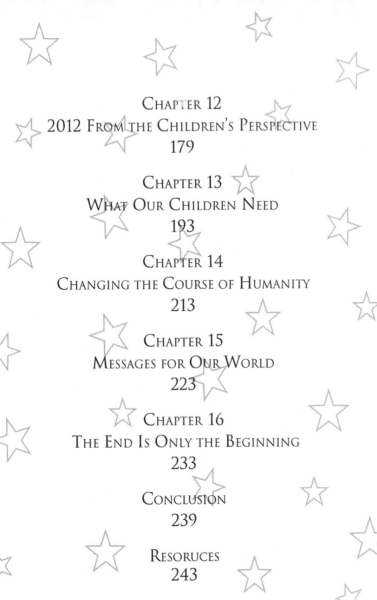

FOREWORD

This book has been written by children! They are very special children, for they represent what many are calling a new consciousness on Earth...an evolvement of humanity that you can see right in the minds of the youngest humans alive. Is it possible? Could we actually be evolving as a human race? If we are, then you are going to see it first in the kids, and in this book.

In the last decade, much has been written about all these new children with the many categories and new names. Education is beginning to fail due to the establishment's unwillingness to bend with this fact, and the drug companies are making a fortune on Ritalin™. Pediatricians are denying this evolvement because it isn't in their textbooks or past experience; meanwhile, more and more children are dropping out of school or being drugged due to a 100-year-old education system that is not addressing an obvious new consciousness.

Meg Blackburn Losey is at the forefront of the exposure of these kids, with the core resources...the children themselves. With permission from their parents, she has given you a book that lets you wander into their minds and see what they are thinking, and in the process lets you decide for yourself if the children of this planet are changing.

Get ready for some unexpected wisdom, poetry, and even glimpses into another world, while these children give answers to profound questions: What is our purpose? Who is God? What happens when you die? Have you been alive before? Are there other dimensions? These children are our future, so get a glimpse of what is coming...read on!

Lee Carroll
Coauthor of *The Indigo Children*

INTRODUCTION

You might be expecting cute child stories in this book. On the contrary, you will find great wisdom on these pages that will make you smile, bring tears to your eyes, make you wonder, challenge your entire belief system, and ultimately awe and inspire you. At least that is our goal, the children and mine. The children who participated in this work did so voluntarily with the permission of their families.

They have a lot to say, and this is just a sampling. There are thousands, if not millions, of these amazing children in our world today, and they are part of a great evolution in the consciousness of humanity.

There is currently an awakening of consciousness unparalleled to any we have witnessed in previous generations, and our children are living testaments to all of this.

What is presently occurring is a startling phenomenon; we have begun to progress into a fast-forward evolution. The intricate inner workings of our DNA are changing, and our brains are beginning to function more fully than ever before. Brain-wave relationships are spontaneously moving into higher vibrational patterning as the electromagnetic fields within our DNA. Because of this, our brains are working together as cohesive units of consciousness. That means humanity is becoming more aware and moving toward becoming sentient beings—aware of everything all at once all of the time.

As described in my previous book, *The Children of Now*, this evolutionary process has many faces amongst our children.

The Indigos were the first to appear. They are the paradigm busters, knowing that the rules of our society are self-serving only to a few, and that the human spirit cannot be controlled with untruth. They are artful beings who are willing to stand up and say no when faced with situations that they feel to be untrue.

The Crystalline Children are sensitive beings who are often telepathic, have natural healing abilities, are perceptive beyond our imaginings, and are here on Earth as representatives of who we once were.

The Star Kids are highly intelligent beings whose DNA segments from our root races and have become active. They are focused on technologies, have innate understandings of energy, and will be the scientists of our future.

Our Transitional Children are neither Indigo nor Crystalline, but have mixed sets of energies. They are often gifted in their own rights, but unwilling or able to display those gifts. Instead, they begin to believe that they are "different," not of value, or just plain weird. These kids often become involved in drugs, alcohol, violence, or worse.

The Beautiful Silent Ones are a niche of humanity who, in my perception, are the most endearing. Generally with physical dysfunction that runs the gamut from minor to the extreme, these children cannot, or do not, speak. Instead, their voices are telepathic, and some people are beginning to hear them.

Categorizing these children was never my intention; however, during countless hours of working with them and their families I began to notice obvious trends, and how the children in each of these groups seemed to have specific traits. In order to fully communicate this growing phenomenon I found vocabulary to differentiate. I still maintain that labeling children is not the way to go, as it makes them feel as if they are an aside from humanity, when in fact they are the very truth of who we are.

So, *why is this evolution happening*?

Overall, we live in the illusion that we are each individual entities and different from all others. While in some respects that is true, the flip side is that we are all created of the same substance as all of creation. We are created of God, the Source, the Creator, Light—whatever we choose to call it, and we are one in a much more intricate picture than our thinking minds can comprehend.

The truth is, as the human race, we have forgotten who we are and of what we are capable. We have deluded ourselves into believing that we are the most important manifested beings in all of creation. We look at other people and judge them, we judge ourselves by what others do, and we measure our accomplishments by what we see others doing. We feel empty, as if something is missing in our world.

Our religions battle over what truths they feel we should be allowed to believe when in fact those truths were modified centuries ago, alleviating most of the ancient texts and translating just a few others to fit what was wanted at the time. As we have found, there was a lot left out concerning the discovery of the Nag Hammadi Gospels and other ancient scrolls found in the Middle East.

There are many holes in the information we have regarding the history of humanity. There is archeological evidence of human existence more than a million years ago.

There is evidence of technology that is far beyond anything we know today, existing in what I like to call "the before times." Before human history.

In ancient Egypt, pyramids, which to this day awe and inspire us, were built by people who had only primitive technology. The pyramids have withstood abuse from deluges, floods, sandstorms, and unthinkable events on Earth, overall showing little wear.

The Sumerians wrote of the people who came from another planet and had advanced technologies. Their other writings consist of what sounds like a nuclear explosion, possibly what the Bible describes as Sodom and Gomorrah. The Sumerian tablets also speak of those visitors interbreeding with human beings.

In India, ancient texts refer to flying machines called *vimana* that carried people all over the Earth. We even see those flying machines pictured in ancient art, high in the background as if flying machines were a normal occurrence at the time. Of course we all know that no one knew how to fly back then, right?

The old writings also talk about other mysteries of technology that we, as perceived advanced societies, have yet to discover. There is more about human history that is denied than there is deemed acceptable. The point is, somewhere inside of us, there are stored innate memories of our entire history—cellular memory that contributes to our instincts.

Early on we learned to protect ourselves from predators and enemies as we began to migrate seasonally in ancient times, looking for food, water, and shelter. We began to interact with other beings with the means of trading and marrying, among other things. Instead of simple survival reactions, our minds learned the art of subtlety. We began to think, and as we did, we closed the doors to our higher knowing, our conscious awareness that was accessed by higher vibrational brain waves, gamma waves, and even finer frequencies that we rode into universal reality.

As a result, we developed egos that became our governor, holding us back, weighing our experiences against previous ones. We evolved into fearful people with perceptions that we were separate from each other. We became mentally oriented, and that served us to a point.

Now, we are evolving full circle. Spontaneously, many adults have begun to awaken to a greater reality, knowing that there is much more to our existence than we previously perceived. As we adults have begun that awakening, we have become bridges for the progression of consciousness in humanity. With that awakening, we have given birth to new generations of children who bring to us messages that we have long forgotten. They remember everything, or at least large enough pieces of our past, to give it not only credibility, but life.

The children's messages are pure in form and sentiment. During the time that I have worked with children and their families, they have told me story after story about fantastic journeys, technologies, multidimensional awareness, their observations of humanity, God, our world, and everything in between.

As *The Children of Now* has traveled around the world, many of the readers have shared even more stories with me. Honestly, this stuff was too beautiful, too important to just remain in my notes.

For the purpose of this work, I devised a series of questions that seem to be the most prevalent topics for which humanity seeks clarity. As adults, we strive to understand the less tangible aspects of our existence. We want to know who we are and from where we came. We want to know why we are here.

We disagree over whose God is the only God, and live our lives based upon what we think our perfect God wants us to do. This, of course, is based upon our religious teachings and values, which have been handed down for generations. We wonder who God really is and what that means to us, and sometimes those beliefs don't sit right inside of us. We begin to question.

We talk about unconditional love, but do we really *know* what love is? I wanted to find out what the children, unfettered by adult senses, had to say.

We wonder if there is life beyond our reality, and strive to leave our bodies, if for nothing more than a glimpse of "out there" to see if it is indeed real. And then, if and when we do get "there," it frightens many of us into leaving behind that which we saw, heard, or felt. For others, this serves as an opening door to greater realities.

We spend much of our lives fearing death, as if it is something that can be avoided. We don't really know or remember what is next, and we battle the duality of our humanity and our higher awareness, which suggests that just maybe there is not only life after death, but life beyond our here and now.

Wars occur every day of our lives for some reason or another, usually over religious issues, boundary issues, or some commodity that would make one group wealthier and more powerful than the others.

We want to find ways to save our world as we deplete her resources. Often we treat our planet with indifference of the privileged, forgetting that it is from the body of our planet that most of our comfort comes, and those resources are limited.

There is much talk and speculation about the coming year of 2012. Will the world end? Will there be serious changes on Earth? Are the coming times about a much greater possibility, a leap of human consciousness? Or is this whole concern really about nothing at all?

I decided to ask the children about *everything*. They share wisdom beyond belief on an everyday basis with off-hand profundities. People think they are being cute, but the truth is that they know. *They know*.

The questions I ask pull no punches, and are dead on with the pertinent issues in the hearts and minds of ongoing humanity. I wanted the children to have the opportunity to speak out of their own volition. And speak out they have. My comments are very few as the children talk about their experiences. In no way did I want to lead them or encourage them into fanciful answers. In order to keep it clean, I played the observer, gently providing the direction I wanted, and then allowing them to take the answers wherever they wanted. There were times I might have, could have, probed even deeper, and perhaps at another time I will. My intention was to keep this conversation relative to the questions at hand.

I have to say that I am in awe of the children who participated in this project. As I read their answers, I was at once humbled and filled with wonder at their perceptions of the intangible and their outright frankness. Honestly, I laughed and I cried.

Common threads began to develop in interview after interview, and it seems that the collective consciousness of the children has a message for humanity. I offer these messages to you here, from the Children of Now.

Just before each chapter, I have set aside sections that I lovingly deemed "the wisdom pages." On each of these is a quote or two from the children that pertains to the chapter. If nurtured and allowed to be who they are, these children are going to take our world to places we have never imagined.

Another wonderful and unexpected occurrence during the interview process was that several of the children spontaneously contributed their art and poetry, some of which, with their permission, and their parent's permission, I have included throughout this writing.

It has been an honor and a privilege to work with each of these wondrous beings, along with their parents and caregivers, and to offer to you, the reader, the heartfelt possibility that our children remind us that it is never too late to be who we are, to live mutually with regard for all others, to love fully, to let go of our fear of things we just don't understand, and infinite other possibilities that are available to us because we *are* the change that we seek. Just listen to the kids....

Blessings, Grace, and Peace.
Meg Blackburn Losey, Msc.D., Ph.D.

1

Know thyself and you know the universe.

That is such a great thing because if you
know yourself you can combat anything that
comes at you.

And anybody can call you a name or
something like that

and it won't really matter because you know
who you are.

It's kind of like water going over a rock.

If you know yourself you can be a really
strong rock.

Who are *you* Scotty?

"I am *definitely* a strong rock."

—Scotty

MEET *the* CHILDREN

How can I express the wonder that I felt as I came to know each of these brilliant hearts? In their innocence, each has offered some glint of light into a world that many have forgotten, as well as the suggestion that there are choices and infinite possibilities available to us.

Some of the children have chosen to bring their gifts into the world in a public way. Others choose to remain more private, touching those in their everyday circles with the love of the infinite.

Wherever possible, the children have written their own biographies; others are written by their parents.

Each child is a magnificent mirror for humanity. They will teach us love and beyond! It is my honor and privilege to introduce the major participants in this work.

NICHOLAS TSCHENSE

Many of you may remember Nicholas's awe-inspiring foreword in *The Children of Now*. Nicholas Tschense is an enchanting 10-year-old boy who has a mission in life! At 3 years old, he said, "Listen up, I have a tremendous purpose in life I am here to teach God (our Creator) messages."

His dream is to reach more than 10,000,000 people in the next few years and teach them about unconditional love. His teachings are pure and simple. Nicholas's words resonate a power of truth that can set any heart free. Through the years he has had many accomplishments due to his gift of understanding the meaning of pure love.

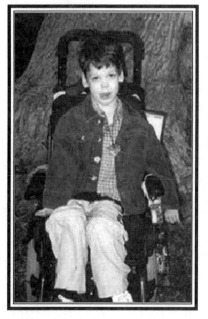

Nicholas began to write inspirational poetry at the early age of 3 with his first poem entitled "Rare Beauty," which was about a tree. Since then, he has authored a book called *Nicholas Inspires God's Love for All*. Nicholas also had the distinct and unusual honor of being a guest speaker at many international events, with his first appearance being at the age of 5. At that time, he received the first Child and Youth Award for Healing and Peace.

At the age of 6, Nicholas was invited by James Twyman to Ashland, Oregon, to share his message of peace at a conference.

As word about Nicholas continues to rapidly spread, he is most celebrated for his honor of being appointed a Love Ambassador for The Love Foundation.

Nicholas expresses that even though his physical challenges can slow him down, there is no lingering when it comes to teaching people about love. To learn more about this mesmerizing little boy who is captivating hearts everywhere, visit his Website at *www.friendsofnicholas.com*.

JUDE DECOFF

My name is Jude. I was born in Landsthul, Germany, on October 27, 1981. In numerology this makes my life path an 11. In short, 11 represents the qualities of a teacher, guide, mentor, illuminator of enlightenment, and many other very notable words that point to the master number and a life of highly charged energies.

My father's name is Jude as well, which makes me a junior. This proves to everyone that I was not named after the famous Beatles song. I was named after my father, who was named after St. Jude, the saint of hopeless causes.

The reason for this name was because my grandmother was unable to have children until the day that she prayed to this last-resort saint, and then was blessed with four children in a row.

My mother's name was Joanne Knight. I use her maiden name, because other than applying for credit cards and student loans, I do not know her. I was taken away from her when I was 3 years old, along with my sister Jennifer. We were physically, emotionally, and sexually abused during our time with our birth mother. My grandmother Marie Clair Deshaes DeCoff, who died from colon cancer six years ago; my grandfather Joseph DeCoff Sr.; and my father, raised us until my father remarried Carolyn Anne Rotti when I was 12 years old.

I attended David Prouty Regional High School in Spencer, Massachusetts, and graduated with honors as a member of the National Honor Society when I was 17. In my senior year of high school I attended Worcester State College as a part of the dual enrollment program for advanced students. I then attended The University of Massachusetts in Amherst, Massachusetts. I graduated with a Bachelors of Arts in communication and minors in psychology and comparative religions. It took me about seven years to finally graduate.

I completed my certification in grief and paranormal counseling in 2007. I also have my Massachusetts bartender's license and am going to be taking the state Realtor's exam prior to December 2007.

With all of this behind me, I have almost completed my biography titled *Through Indigo Eyes*, which will hopefully be published soon.

I have been working in the hotel industry for the last five years; however, I would like to pursue my psychic career more in depth. I have an office in Northampton, Massachusetts, in my friend's store called Sacred Endeavors LLC. I conduct Oracle card readings, teach workshops on Numerology and card readings, hold grief counseling sessions, and counsel others in life management along with the metaphysical and psychic sides of their lives. My office opened in May 2007, and is slowly gaining speed. I began my practice by selling my readings on eBay™. (From Dr. Meg: Jude's readings are extensive and *accurate*!)

With all these things going on in my life, I was synchronistically asked by the author of this book to contribute. I knew that this would be a once-in-a-lifetime chance to get my messages out to the world, and to finally reach the broad audience (that as an 11 of enlightenment), for which I had hoped.

I plan to move to Parker, Arizona, around October 2007. The reason for this is so I can move closer to the planetary alignment of my Pluto line, which is my psychic ley line that runs from Las Vegas, Nevada, and all points directly north and south. If you would like to know more about me, I would be more than happy to answer questions through my e-mail at jtdecoff1027@hotmail.com, or you can read my up-and-coming biography, *Through Indigo Eyes*.

Grandma Chandra

"Grandma" Chandra says that we are ready for contact with other dimensions. We must lift the veils from our faces and go beyond the physical.

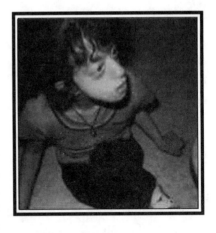

Grandma Chandra, a living miracle, is an Omni-Dimensional being in a severely physically challenged body. Due to her physical challenges, Grandma has other gifts. She appears whole and complete in people's dream or meditation states, where she urges them to contact her so she can assist in awakening them to their True Whole Selves.

At 3 months old, Chandra began doing "mudras" with her fingers—these are sacred signs for Universal Intelligence and OM.

At 9 1/2 years old, Chandra started doing spontaneous past-life readings with everyone she came into contact with. Not bound by the body, Chandra has unbroken past-life recall.

Grandma Chandra's life has been an amazing series of awakenings and events, during which she has shared her phenomenal gifts with the world.

At 16, Chandra was given the title "Grandma" by Native American Chief Golden Eagle, who recognized her as an original pipe carrier, or wisdom bearer.

At 17, it was discovered that Chandra reads through her fingertips by spinning papers, closed books, magazines, and so on. She can then tell you a page in a book and how it pertains to you or someone else in the room. She does this with various spiritual/sacred books and papers when she does readings for people.

James Twyman, international peacemaker and author of *Emissary of Light* and *Emissary of Love* discovered Chandra when she was 19. Grandma Chandra was invited as a presenter to his Psychic Indigo Children Conference in Kona, Hawaii. After this conference, Chandra began coding people according to their planetary mission and how to achieve it.

At 20, Chandra asserts that she is a 12th-dimensional being who has come here to guide and teach those whose codes she activates with her readings and CD, "The Awakening Codes of Grandmother Chandra."

Grandma had e-mail communication with the grandson of Jacques Cousteau; she asked if she could have a tape of the whales at 35,000 feet deep. He replied that the ocean is only 25,000 feet deep. Chandra disagreed, and he replied by asking if she was talking about a trench. She replied, "Yes, it is in the South Pacific." She subsequently received a CD of the whales at 35,000 feet, and has translated the message of the whales to us in her CD, "Whalespeak."

In May of 2003, Chandra said that she is a "Star Gate opener." She began opening Star Gates during her presentations around the United States. Star Gates are nonphysical portals, gates, doorways, and openings around the planet that allow only the highest vibratory Ascended Masters, Angels, and Guides, including extraterrestrials to come and assist us and the planet in advancing to the next conscious level of Peace and Ascension. Chandra said, "If we do not ask them, they cannot come even though we all have contracted to awaken to our codes and allow them to assist us. We must ask." This is the purpose of Star Gate openings.

In July 2003, Chandra reunited with Jimmy Twyman in Ashland, Oregon, for his second Psychic Indigo Children Conference. There she spoke of the need for all of us to do our planetary mission, for "time" as we know it is speeding up.

In November 2003, Grandma hosted a Harmonic Concordance presentation in Scottsdale, Arizona, helping people awaken to their planetary missions.

In February 2004, Grandma took part in the Sacred Geometry Conference in Sedona, Arizona, speaking about the axitonal lines of the subtle body and their relationship to sacred geometry.

In June 2004, Grandma went to Holland for presentations and workshops. There she developed the Grandma Chandra Attunement Chamber, an Omni-Dimensional manifestation chamber that helps us to recover lost parts of ourselves due to being taken by extraterrestrials willingly or unwilling for experiments or teaching.

In November 2004, Grandma flew to Taos, New Mexico, to assist Chief Golden Eagle (aka Black Spotted Horse) on the energies of the 11:11 phenomenon that promote changes in the Earth's morphogenetic field.

In December 2004, Grandma again allied with Chief Golden Eagle for a 12:12 presentation in Sedona, Arizona, where she spoke of the 12th dimension and how to access it.

In March 2005, Grandma pointed to a local map and said we must buy a house there. She chose the house by the Star Gate in its living room, and we moved there at the end of May. She said that this is a "stepping stone" house to be used to start her "Awakening Center of Grandma Chandra."

In June of 2005, Grandma went to Los Angeles for a presentation at the Earth and Sky Lodge. While there, she telepathed with some highly placed musicians and told them that it is time for her to create a DVD on the "sounds of the planets." One of the musicians taped her drumming and said, "She is drumming the sounds of the spheres according to the Pythagorean theorem." (Source: JB, Los Angeles.)

To find out more, visit Grandma on her Website at *www.grandmachandra.com.*

TRISTAN

Tristan Boardway, also known as "Trevor" in *The Children of Now*, is 13 years old and lives with his mom, dad, and three dogs, Haley, Holly, and Latte.

During his life, Tristan has exhibited many special gifts, including telepathic communication, seeing auras, remembering past lives as well as future lives, and communicating with spirits, aliens, and other interesting beings. He can also sense other's emotional and physical pain, and sends healing energy to those areas. Because of his sensitivities, it is sometimes overwhelming for Tristan to feel so much of the energy from others. Because of this, he has learned many grounding exercises to help him feel more comfortable. Tristan is still working on balancing his energy.

Crawling and walking were quite difficult for Tristan, and he always seemed quite foreign in his body. Through the help of many alternative modalities, he has overcome those steps and is now an amazing skier, leaving his dad in the dust! For Tristan, speaking has been another area that has not come so easily; perhaps this is because he is telepathic. He didn't begin speaking until he was about 3 years old, and as he did, his speech was very unclear and fragmented. Now at 13, his mom can testify to the fact that he talks nonstop, as well as asks unlimited questions. Although Tristan's speech is still not quite as clear as it could be, he has no problem expressing himself to others, and is very social.

Tristan has been homeschooled all his life, and enjoys learning about subjects such as the universe; the space program; indigenous cultures; ancient civilizations; anatomy; history; geography; geometry; and of course, any topic about animals.

He has always been interested in flying, so he has studied everything he can find on the flight and space programs. His favorite test pilot is Chuck Yeager, who broke the sound barrier in the Bell-X1. Tristan was always interested in becoming an astronaut until he saw the training videos of the spinning chair. Since that time, he is even more determined to figure out how he can get his physical body to fly again like it did when he was in spirit form.

Some of the activities he enjoys are skiing, swimming, hiking, and karate. Tristan has learned Reiki Level 1 and will soon be learning Reiki Level 2. Currently, he is learning Level 1 Springforest Qigong.

Presently, Tristan is investigating the idea of training one of his dogs to become a Delta Dog, so they can visit the residents at the local convalescent hospital.

SCOTTY

(Scotty has asked that we do not use his photo or full name for his privacy.)

My name is Scotty and I am 15 years old. I have known what I was going to do on this planet since I was put here! I am here to change the world.

Ever since I was little, I have always felt as if I was light-years ahead of my teachers and the other adults around me.

I constantly have dreams of the future and of me helping and saving people. A lot of the time I wake up tired because I am literally working all night. I am a dream walker, and in my dreams I am on a whole new plane.

I can continuously see the future and what is going to happen. Somehow my mind works like a symbol encyclopedia: what I see in my dreams and in my work are symbols, but my mind can read them as if they are words.

Many other beings visit me in meditation and sleep, and they are constantly helping me figure out this word and myself. To know thyself is to know the universe.

JASIN (JACOB) FURMAN

You might remember Jasin from *The Children of Now* as "Craig." His real name is Jake, but recently he decided to change that. For now, he chooses "Jasin." On the surface, Jasin is a typical boy with an amazing ability to integrate into society. He has taken on the role of a human boy born on December 11, 1999, in Paradise Valley, Arizona. He is in the second grade and excels in school. He has won awards for science, math, and writing. But don't let this fool you. Jasin is anything but typical.

As an infant, Jasin's parents noticed little things, such as electronic toys playing in the middle of the night when he was in his crib, as well as playing with toys while he was across the room and saying, "I did that." After noticing that not all humans are aware of this ability, Jasin says that he filed this ability in a drawer, and will go to that drawer when he is ready.

Jasin has mentioned a few things that make us realize that, as infants, these beings are born with total recall—and they retain this memory. Jasin was recently telling a story of when he was an infant. Remembering it as if it were yesterday, he described his crib as, "...this cage I used to sleep in." After recovering from the shock, his mother explained that it was not a cage, but his bed. He remarked that it was like a jail cell, but now he understands that it's just the way things are done here.

This is just a drop in the bucket. He can recount some past lives here on Earth. He visits other dimensions. He can remote view. Often, while driving along the cliff areas in Sedona, Arizona, he tells of Natives that were ambushed. If asked when it happened, he will say in a deep voice, with eyes black as coal, "It was in the time of the Ottoman." He gets homesick for his planet. He sometimes goes off into a trance and makes comments about things that are not in balance at home. He says that he is like a king there, and his people need him. He seems to have the ability to bilocate in these times.

There is a beauty in the way Jasin sees life. While looking at the flame of a candle at night, he marvels in the glowing light—not the flame. He can find the magic in beetles and snakes, and can hear the whisper of the wind. He can sit silently on the edge of the Grand Canyon and know that it is proof that God is there. He says that when you are at a site that was painted by God, you can hear him speaking.

Jasin is a living example of a loving being. When told the old saying, "find a penny, pick it up, all day long you'll have good luck," he took matters into his own hands. He spent an entire day placing pennies in obscure places during his mother's daily errands. He continues to place pennies around wherever he goes. His reasoning is that he is making the world a happier place. It makes his heart glow to know that someone will smile when they find those pennies. He knows that he is making a difference, one smile at a time. Additionally, he is always 10 steps ahead of most people. Earlier this year, he asked his grandmother from New Jersey to send him a specific toy. Well—the toy just sits there on his shelf. In fact there are a few toys that just sit there. This sounds pretty typical for a 7 year old, right? Being aware that Jasin does nothing randomly, his mother asked him why he wanted these toys if he was not going to play with them. He said, "I plan on packing them into the donation pile that we do just before Christmas. Kids that have less toys would really appreciate having one of these, but their parents can't give them much stuff. I'd rather let them have a nice Christmas."

Jasin's parents moved to a 6-acre parcel in the Prescott National Forest two years ago. They noticed that Jasin is happiest when there are trees and open space around him. The city life literally shuts him down and makes him agitated. Every time he saw construction and destruction, it was very

emotional for him. Now, when taking him to the more popu-
lated areas, Jasin's parents remind him to stay grounded. Jasin
spends his days with his animals and Guides. He has chosen
to be schooled in a Virtual Academy so that he can explore
life without the societal games. He likes that he has study
time away from the general public, but still sets play dates
with his friends. Though he would not admit it, he quietly
holds space for his mother while she sees clients in their home.

Jasin has gathered a small group of Crystalline and Star
Children as playmates. His mother recounts a time when two
of the children were discussing how things are in the new dimension. They were actually making fun of this one, like it was
a cartoon written for toddlers. While giggling, she heard them
say, "yeah, like the new sun is clear light, not all yellow like
this one"). Another friend sees into the past, when Natives
gathered in loin clothes for a party in what is now Jasin's backyard. One tells of having spirits that speak to him. But for the
most part, they just play, laugh, and have fun! In fact—that is
what they enjoy the most.

Jasin is not the typical boy. He is present, guided, and driven.
His mother frequently needs to remind him that he came this
time around to be the kid, and that he needs to allow his parents the role of parent. This is a delicate balance for all concerned. He knows what he wants and how to get it. He knows
who he is and how to be. He has come here for a purpose and
understands that it is important. As mentioned before, he recently changed his name. He wants to now be called Jasin, and
he wants it to be spelled this way. He knows that the sound of
his name is important, and that Jasin fits him. This was not
discussed beforehand. He woke up at 7 a.m. on 07/07/07 and
heard the name Jasin. He looked at himself in the mirror and
said, "That fits me." He then woke his mother at 7:15 am and
announced that he would like to be called Jasin from now on.
His other name doesn't fit him—it doesn't sound right. Sensing the importance, his parents were very supportive. A few
days later, his mother looked the name up. Jasin means "healer."

GABRIEL

(Written by Gabriel's mom)

Gabriel is 11 years old. He is a very, very small child as eating is very difficult for him. He reads and builds things and spends most of his time alone. At school he wanders, and does

not connect to the other kids because he says he cannot play their games; they have an edge of meanness that hurts his heart and head.

Gabriel's teachers report that he is the most respected kid in class, as he always has very insightful things to say, and is always kind.

When he was an infant he spent hours looking at the trees and moving his hand in front of the images. When words started to come he told me he saw beautiful people in the trees and was sad I could not see them.

At 2 1/2 years old, he helped a dog through her death by telling us things the dog needed. Some of those things did not seem right, but when we tried it the dog responded exactly as he said she would. After a day of nursing this dog, he held the dog (who had never let other kids near her) and told her not to be afraid. He told her that she could go "bye-bye," and she died in his arms.

At the age of 3, Gabriel told me that he remembered being designated to come back to this planet when I called him, but he said he missed the light after he left.

Gabriel would report to me that his friends were experiencing trauma even before anyone else knew.

We do not speak of Angels a great deal, but whenever we do, Gabriel initiates the conversation.

We have tried a variety of churches, and he usually leaves, moved to tears at the relationship to God, yet telling me that each church we have attended is not his soul's home.

Gabriel is lonely, but is very clear about the fact that he could never be anything other than what he is. We work regularly on Gabriel's greatest concern: that he will not be able to give everything that he knows he is supposed to give in this lifetime.

That I can be near him everyday is a gift in my life.

I sometimes worry I am not big enough to hold the enormity of his heart.

AHN (JASMINE)

(Written by her mother)

Jasmine Ahn Caldwell van Mentz (her preferred name being Ahn van Mentz) was born to an inter-racial couple on June 18, 1992, in western Washington. She was a lively, alert, and happy toddler with high curiosity and sensitivity. Her signature "buddy" was Curious George, and one of her nicknames was "Buddha" (not sure why, it just suited her). At age 3, Ahn began speech therapy in preschool due to the fact that she had a speech delay. While other children her age were chattering up a storm, Ahn was a girl of few words. She understood words, but was not verbal herself. One pediatrician suggested it

might be because she had an older sister who could do all the talking for her, and so she didn't need to talk. That proved not to be the reason, however.

Ahn was a feisty child, and during preschool got very upset if she couldn't be the "line leader." One preschool teacher handled this very well by allowing her to choose who would be the line leader—brilliant idea! When you choose someone to lead, you can't very well be upset when they do.

Ahn represents a person with a different way of being. This was evident early on, yet in such a subtle way that she, being a round peg, was still being forced to fit into the square hole desired and required by society.

Ahn's hearing was so sensitive that when her family took her to the movies, she would cry unless she wore earmuffs to muffle the sounds. Ahn's sensitivities did not end with her acute hearing. Being an Empath, she picks up on what everyone around her is feeling. This can be a great gift, unless the empathic person gets lost in those feelings and doesn't know what belongs to others and what belongs to them. Life in the school environment was overly stimulating, distracting, and exhausting for Ahn. She did her best to function in it; however, it took a toll on her physical body.

Ahn started her prolific writing at age 11 after her parents divorced. She moved from the big city to a small town in Canada. Ahn's sister was in college at the time, and she felt a great need to let out her feelings, so she started writing poems and lyrics. She seemed to pull words from the Universe, often not knowing the meaning of some of the words, and put them on paper. These words often had double meanings, and were insightful and profound. Her mother was amazed and especially touched by two of her first poems: "Mother Angel" and "Cement Cage."

Sometimes Ahn's way of being would really challenge adults and the normal ways things were done. ADHD was suspected as she struggled to focus and fit in. Being extra sensitive to energy, Ahn would refuse to enter a place with fluorescent lighting. Going to the mall (which most teenagers would love to do) could make her feel physically ill. Learning techniques to center and ground became critical so the anxiety created from her extreme sensitivity to people and her environment did not overtake her.

She chose, at age 14, to limit her interaction with her peers and was homeschooled. She is a visual and "hands-on" learner. Ahn found a routine that included yoga, meditation, regular massage and energy work, and working with the Angels. She discovered the positive effect that nature, especially water, had on her, and the benefits of being around trees, rocks, crystals, and animals. Also, she discovered the importance of high vibrational music and lyrics, high vibrational food and drink, plus movement and dance. Her passion, which pushes her from the inside, is creating and performing. She is super-sensitive to the vibrations of words and sounds. She is currently developing her skills in toning; singing; playing the harp, the drums, and other musical instruments.

Ahn often finds it difficult being in the physical, and remembers being in spirit—"a blob of pure love-energy floating in space." She would prefer to use her skills of telepathy and remote viewing—tapping into the galactic grid of consciousness. She often does this in her dream state.

Ahn has a deeply rooted desire for harmony and truth, yet if integrity is missing in a situation, her warrior spirit comes out, and she is willing to set aside the harmony to expose the truth. Ahn is dedicated to leading with her heart, standing in her power and truth, and inspiring others to do the same through her creative works and life. Her current favorite recording artist is India Arie, and two of her favorite authors are Doreen Virtue and Eckhart Tolle. She chooses to live by the motto brought forth from Mahatma Gandhi, "Be the change you want to see in the world!"

And a few words from Ahn:

> Poetry and lyrics sort of flow out of me, and to share them with others, I am creating a Website that will be up soon. My Website will be called "BlueStarLight." I know one of my animal totems is the "spider," and I used to have a great fear of them. When I was 12, it came to me that my fear of spiders was really a fear of my own power and creativity (the spider represents creativity and magic with the written word).

> I have many plans, including a clothing line using the tarantula on my label. Singing and dancing are my passions. I also love playing musical instruments (especially the harp), and I'm interested in sound healing. I desire to use my gifts to enlighten others, to be in JOY, and to help create our New Earth full of unconditional LOVE.

CHRISTINA MARIE SIEGL

(Written by her mother, Margi)

Christina was born on March 25, 1990.

She was my second child. As little sisters will do, Christina followed her older sister around constantly. If there was only one of something—like in a set of toys—the sisters squabbled over it, but the next day, there would be two of that thing. I would ask where the second toy came from, and Christina would say, "I made it with my magic." We lived way up in the mountains, so there was no place for her to get another toy, but there it would be.

Christina has always been very sensitive and can communicate with animals, which I think helps her in dressage, but she can also communicate with animals remotely. She is going to start showing a 17-hand Oldenberg mare this fall in dressage.

Everyone is attracted to Christina, especially those who are hurting; she is like a magnet for them. She is often the one who is confided in by her peers. She always tries to help, but sometimes the problems they bring to her are a little overwhelming. I think that is why she didn't like high school.

Christina has been told she has ADD because she seems distracted a lot, but she just says that is when she is tuned in to the other side and is receiving information.

For a long time she insisted she had "only seen one Angel!" But after her first Eden event (a yearly event that is centered around Angels), she sees them all the time. Christina had an amazing experience after a ceremony at the event. She was able to visit my late father, but had to go out on the boat to visit him, because he couldn't come ashore.

Christina was often sick as a younger child, and, as a result, missed a lot of school. Despite this, she always understood the material and could ace the tests, but she had poor grades from not turning in her homework. She felt it was just "busywork." I think she channeled a lot of the answers on tests. I actually had someone ask me if that counted as cheating! She is 17 years old and has just finished her first year at a community college.

When Christina was in middle school, I found out that she often went out of body and visited her dragons. It was how she saw her Guardians. I think she started doing that when things were difficult for her.

Christina likes to communicate with me telepathically, but gets frustrated when I don't receive her messages fully. She is a wonderfully gentle person and a delight to be around.

PETER DONALD SIEGL

(Written by his mother, Margi)

After Christina was born, the doctors recommended I have a hysterectomy. I refused, but I couldn't tell them it was because my son wasn't here yet. He had come to me before I became pregnant, and told me he was coming to help heal his father. He said he would have hazel eyes and hair darker than Julia's, but lighter than Christina's. Julia is a blue-eyed blond, and Christina is a dark-eyed brunette.

My pregnancy with Peter was difficult, with several episodes of early labor. On July 19, 1993, Peter was born very small, and for a time was considered a "failure-to-thrive baby." He has sure made up for that—he is well over 6 feet tall and still growing!

I always said he caused all his trouble before he was born. He has always been the sweetest, kindest boy I have ever known. He went in to the principal's office every day when he was in first grade and insisted he needed to "help the poor." He didn't let up until she let him organize a food drive at school; I did not know about this until after the flyers were printed.

One day he came home very upset because a boy had punched him several times. I asked him what he had done and his response was: "I walked away. Violence isn't the answer, Mom!"

Another time he was very upset and couldn't calm down. I had tried everything and eventually said maybe his Angels could help. He calmed down quickly, and I asked if that helped. He said it did. Then I asked if he could see his Angels and he gave me this incredulous look. He said something along the lines of, "Well duh! Of course I can SEE them!!" He had never mentioned this before. When I asked more about them he said they came to check in on him. When I asked what they were doing he said, "Just hanging there in the air."

During a ceremony in which Peter participated, he said four Angels came to him and each was bearing a gift. The Angels brought him health, beauty, strength, and love. They were standing in front of a large door, which they said he could enter if he came back sometime.

Peter has brought me so much joy.

JOSEPH

We knew from an early age that Joseph was special, and he seemed to have an understanding of life that was well beyond his years. When he was just 3 years old, he would tell us that the Angels would come to him at night and tell him about many things. "Like what?" I would ask. Things about love and healing, he would tell me. He stated that he could hear the Angels talking to him from their brain to his brain. No words.

For several years, Joseph seemed to know what would happen in the future. The most remarkable was early on the morning of September 11, 2001, when he told me that two planes were going to hit two tall buildings and lots of people were going to die. A half hour later, the World Trade Center was hit by two planes. Not only do I think he saw all that

happened that day prior to it happening, but I think he also felt the sadness.

He also seemed to remember the past. One time, when we were driving home, he started to tell me about a past life when we were all Indians. When he was only 4 years old, he said he could think back prior to his birth and remember that he decided to come here to Earth. He told me that he can see big circles of colors when he closes his eyes. He called these colors "love and energy." He said when the colors hit your body they heal any damage that is happening.

Today, Joseph is 10 years old. He is an intelligent, articulate, highly sensitive, and passionate boy. School can sometimes be a challenge—not academically, but more with trying to fit into the system. He still shows remarkable abilities. Just this year we were driving home from school and I asked him about his day. He said that during a fourth-grade singing program, he closed his eyes and immediately left his body. He was floating above the children watching the program, and he was able to see lots of colors around the children's bodies. I told him that was pretty cool. He casually responded, "Yea, I guess, other than that, school was okay."

He doesn't understand the reasons for war, poverty, greed, and the abuse of wildlife and nature. He loves Shamanism, mythological creatures, and all nature and wildlife. His favorite saying is:

> *Treat the Earth well.*
> *It was not given to you by your parents.*
> *It was lent to you by your children.*
>
> —Indian Proverb

SCOTT

Scott is 12, but way "older" than his years. He has been collecting crystals for about four years now, and generally loves to collect and build things. Scott loves to make people laugh, and he has a great affinity for animals, especially dogs and cats.

When he was 8 years old, Scott met some of his spirit guides and continues to converse with them on a daily basis. He expects people to do the right thing and obey the rules and laws. He gets very frustrated when people don't. Scott also likes to swim.

WESTON SCHMIER

(Written by his mother, Marilu)

(Weston was one of the stars in *The Children of Now*. There he was known as "William.") Being the parent of Weston has been a lesson in patience as well as faith. Prior to his birth, in a fit of desperate prayer, I believe I was told that I would

have a boy, and that there would be something wrong with him; however, he would be okay eventually. During subsequent prayer, I felt that things would change by the time he was 5 years old. Almost immediately after his birth, we could tell there was something different about him, though doctors' tests revealed nothing concrete. One notable doctor, however, did tell my pediatrician that Weston was severely retarded, and most likely would eventually need to be institutionalized. At approximately 5 1/2 years of age, after years of testing and CT scans, an MRI was done, which revealed a peach-size cyst in his brain. Surgery was performed, and I thought we were on our way to the life I had imagined with him. It was not too long after the surgery that I began seeing Weston in a whole new light.

For a long time, I believed what I was told about Weston and his limitations, as all the experts seemed to agree on that point. Fortunately for us (and this is where faith started to come into the picture), Weston had one professional who put her preconceived notions about him aside and uncovered his ability to read. Because of her I began to see Weston in a new light, and faith started taking over in my communications with him. Soon, I began to realize that maybe he was not retarded, though in the beginning it was very difficult to discount what I had been told for so many years by so many experts. I shared my discovery of his abilities, which, at that time, mostly pertained to academics, with very few people. Within a year or two, I was convinced that it was real, and I began seeing many more of Weston's gifts, including his ability to speak to Angels. It is true that many of my friends have sought his counsel with regard to various issues. One of my favorite memories is when Weston told a friend which college her son would be accepted to a year prior to his taking the SAT, and that he would get accepted on early decision. Sure enough, nine months later that is exactly what happened. It is now commonly accepted amongst friends and family that Weston can speak to Angels and other Divine beings, converse with those who have died, speak to people telepathically, help in determining therapy needs, and so on.

What makes this all amazing is that Weston still does not speak using words. I will ask him questions using a dry-erase board in either a yes/no or multiple-choice format. Sometimes I will ask him about a certain subject throughout a two-week period. I am always astounded that no matter how many different ways I ask a question he always answers the same way. I do believe that one day Weston will speak, but it is my faith that has allowed me to accept Weston for the wonderfully enigmatic boy that he is.

LINDSAY MOORE

I am a 19-year-old student at Agnes Scott College, trying to turn my theatrical passion into a profession, spreading love to whomever I come in contact with, and trying to live this life to the fullest one lesson at a time.

I was born at 2:41 p.m. on February 8, 1988 to Christy Jenkins Moore and Ronald Dean Moore. Looking at the two of them, they seemed quite the odd pair, but I had chosen them and they accepted. My mom had not really known my father in a previous life. As for my father, if it hadn't been for my need to enter into this world, I doubt he would have met my mother. I go way back with both of them, so it seemed appropriate for those two to bring me into being. Their marriage

didn't last much longer after my birth. My only memory of their relationship, which also happened to be my first memory, was lying in between them—my father on the left, my mother on the right, and me squished in the middle, warm and comfy. I am not one of those kids to wish their parents back together...they were not meant for each other, they were just meant for me.

So my childhood was pretty eventful. I decided at the age of 5 that I wanted to chop all of my hair off and be called Scott. Basically I wanted to be a boy. My parents and siblings went along with it. The phase lasted about three months, and at that point I decided to be a tomboy and move on with my life. My sister, who is 25 years my senior, became my second mother, and my two older brothers filmed most of my childhood. All of the embarrassing moments I can't remember are on tape, but that's okay because their embarrassing clothes and funny hairdos are also trapped in time. If you watched these tapes you would think that I was just an average little kid, playing with toys, taking baths in the sink, and singing

"Old McDonald" until my face turned blue. I would later learn at the age of 12 that I was not a "normal" child. I had gifts, ones that I was supposed to use. In sixth grade, after my mom vacationed in Bali while I was at camp, she decided to move us to the mountains so she could open a metaphysical book and gift store. (Lucky me. I had a mother who was going to support me when I came to these major turning points in my life.) I was running around the track at the private school I attended. I was only 12, and it was at that moment I decided to start seeing. I am not sure what prompted this decision. I just stopped running, looked across the empty fields, and said aloud "I'm ready." From that point on my life would not be the same. At first I only saw little woodland creatures with wings dancing around our house. That went on for months. I would talk to them and they would tell me grand stories about their adventures in my backyard, but I knew that this would not last for long. I knew that they were merely preparing me for the next step.

A year later, after only seeing blurs of light and fairies, I was lying in bed one night watching TV and I heard a sort of bang on my window. I pulled up my blinds to find one of the fairies at my window. It was flying excitedly and it began pointing inside my room. I turned around and saw a man sitting at my computer chair. He was slumped casually in the seat, with a wide grin on his face; for some reason I did not freak out. Most people would be a little scared if they turned around to see an unknown man, who looked like a 1920s mobster, sitting in their room. However, he was a familiar face, a friendly face; one I had known my whole life. I lost track of time, but for what seemed like hours we just sat their in each other's company, neither of us speaking. Finally I broke the silence. "You're Charlie aren't you?" The figure nodded and smiled. We then talked for hours, neither of us saying anything out loud, because we were connected. He was my protector. He had been there when I was born. We discussed past lives and lessons for the future. Then I began asking questions about my ability. Why could I see him and other children couldn't? He simply told me that this was my gift; all people had these abilities, they just have to open themselves. I have and I am.

NATHAN

Nathan is lively, energetic, and loves to make people laugh. He enjoys playing with his friends and likes to play *Star Wars* on his dad's PlayStation™. He also enjoys putting things together and looks forward to play-ing "that game with the stick and the balls"

when baseball season starts. Among his favorite things to col-lect are crystals, and he is particularly drawn to amethyst, quartz, and hematite. Nathan has a keen awareness of energy, both in himself and his surroundings. He also seems to dis-play a talent for self-healing. A hug, a warm bath, or a good rest in a cozy chair are all he needs to recover from just about any ailment.

It appears that Nathan communicates with his guides (or perhaps communicates telepathically), even if he's not able to verbalize the experience. One example that demonstrates this happened on a few occasions last year during his sister's math lessons. Here's how it went:

Mom:	Okay, Rhianna, let's practice some math questions. What is 9 + 8?
Rhianna:	Um, 9 + 8, that's 17?
Mom:	Great! What is 24 - 8?

Rhianna:	24 - 8. 24 - 8.
Nathan:	16! (big grin)
Mom:	Wow, Nathan! That's right! Okay, Rhianna, what is 10 - 2?
Nathan:	8! (giggle)
Rhianna:	Nathan, stop!!!
Mom:	Alright, Nathan, let's give Rhianna a turn now!

RHIANNA

Rhianna is an outgoing and compassionate 8-year-old. She enjoys helping others and loves to teach what she knows to the world. Caring for animals and the Earth is very important to her. She also enjoys playing the guitar and singing. One goal she has is to become a singer/songwriter and have her own band. Among Rhianna's spiritual gifts is the ability to see auras and ghosts.

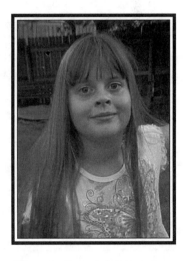

One experience that changed Rhianna happened just a couple of days before this interview; she had been visited by a rather scary individual a few nights in a row. He wore jeans and a belt, but no shirt. His skin was grey, and his face appeared as if it were painted black. He had tattoos all over his body, right up to his neck. (Not a very pleasant sight when you're alone in your room!) At first, Rhianna wasn't sure if it would be a good idea to speak to this spirit, so she asked for her mom's help. With Mom speaking aloud to the spirit and Rhianna relaying his answers, they were able to learn that this person had died almost 30 years ago and needed help. He was afraid to cross over into heaven because he thought God would blame him for the death of his sister. After explaining that God is not vengeful and that his sister was on the other side waiting for him, he began to see a light. He focused on the light and saw his sister. When he spoke to her, the light grew large enough for him to pass through. Just before he crossed over, he thanked Rhianna. Immediately, Rhianna felt a sense of loss, but knew that she had done a tremendous favor to this spirit. As she recalled the event, she also noted that this spirit looked better just before he crossed over into the light—he looked healthier, wore a shirt, and his face was normal. The experience gave her a new respect for ghosts. She is still apprehensive about seeing sprits anywhere other than her home, but she feels that, in time, she would like to help more lost spirits find their way to heaven.

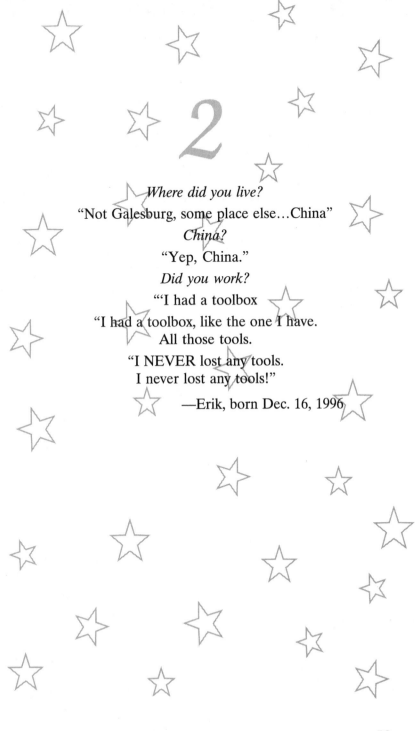

2

Where did you live?

"Not Galesburg, some place else…China"

China?

"Yep, China."

Did you work?

"'I had a toolbox

"I had a toolbox, like the one I have.
All those tools.

"I NEVER lost any tools.
I never lost any tools!"

—Erik, born Dec. 16, 1996

53

CHOOSING LIFE NOW *and* *in the* PAST

Where did we come from? What was it like when we looked out from the heavens and decided when we would come and who we would be? Did some big hand reach down and say, "You! Go there!"? Did we just come into being? Materialize when we were born?

Across the board, whether Crystalline, Star Child, or Indigo, the Children of Now remember past lives, and often prepare and choose to come into this world.

Many of the kids that I have talked with actually remember picking out their parents, choosing them for the challenges that the family unit will present. Some of the children, knowing that they will be different in this life, choose parents who will be able and willing to nurture those differences. The children remember not only the selective process, but entering the body and being born. Usually these memories are forgotten after age 6 or 7, but not always.

The children often talk about their previous lifetimes. The details are frequently staggering, and at times, with some research, verifiable. In *The Children of Now* I talked about one little boy who told his dad that he needed lessons to speak Chinese. Not that he didn't already know it; he just needed help to remember. He was 6 years old. He remembered so many details that his parents researched Chinese history and were actually able to identify who the child had been.

For the purpose of this book, I decided to ask the kids about what they remember. As I encountered one answer after the next, what fascinated me was how the children solidified their different categories by what they remembered. In particular, the Star Children often spoke of memories of distant planets in faraway galaxies. These aren't fanciful notions. These types of memories are a regular occurrence everywhere.

One excellent example of a Star Child's past-life memory was written in a story that was run by Pravda, an online Russian news service. With full permission from Pravda, the following is the story in full. You can also find it at *http:// english.pravda.ru/science/19/94/377/12257_Martian.html*.

BORISKA-BOY FROM MARS
MARCH 12, 2004

Sometimes, some children are born with quite fascinating talents, unusual abilities. I was told the story of an unusual boy named Boriska from members of an expedition to the anomaly zone located in the north of the Volgograd region, most commonly referred to as "Medvedetskaya gryada."

"Can you imagine, while everyone was sitting around the campfire at night, some little boy (about

7 years of age) suddenly asking for everyone's attention? Turned out, he wanted to tell them all about life on Mars, about its inhabitants and their flights to Earth," shares one of the witnesses. Silence followed. It was incredible! The little boy with gigantic, lively eyes was about to tell a magnificent story about the Martian civilization; about megalithic cities, their spaceships and flights to various planets; and about a wonderful country named Lemuria, a life of which he knew in detail since he happened to descend there from Mars, where he had friends.

Logs were cracking, night's fog enveloped the area, and the immense dark sky with myriads of brightly lit stars seemed to conceal some sort of a mystery. His story lasted for about an hour and a half. One guy was smart enough to tape the entire narration.

Many were stunned by two distinct factors. First of all, the boy possessed exceptionally profound knowledge. His intellect was obviously far from that of a typical 7-year-old boy. Not every professor is capable of narrating the entire history of Lemuria, Lemurians, and its inhabitants in such details. You will be unable to find any mention of this country in school textbooks. Modern science has not yet proved existence of other civilizations. We were all amazed by the actual speech of this young boy. It was far from the kind kids his age usually use. His knowledge of specific terminology, details, and facts from Mars's and Earth's past fascinated everyone.

"Why did he start the conversation in the first place," said my interlocutor. "Perhaps he was simply touched by the overall atmosphere of our camp with many knowledgeable and open-minded people," he continued. "Could he make this all up?""Doubtful," objected my friend. "To me this looks more like the boy was sharing his personal memories from past births. It is virtually impossible to make up such stories; one really had to know them.

"Today, after meeting with Boriska's parents and getting to know the boy better, I begin to carefully sort out all the information obtained around that campfire. He was born in Volzhskii in a suburban hospital, even though officially, based on the paperwork, his birthplace is the town of Zhirnovsk of Volgograd region. His birthday is January 11, 1996. (Perhaps it will be helpful for astrologers.) His parents seem to be wonderful people. Nadezhda, Boriska's mother, is a dermatologist in a public clinic. She graduated from Volgograd Medical Institute not so long ago in 1991. The boy's father is a retired officer. Both of them would be happy if someone could shed the light onto the mystery behind their child. In the meantime, they simply observe him and watch him grow."

After Boriska was born, I noticed he was able to hold his head up in 15 days," recalls Nadezhda. "His first word *baba* he uttered when he was 4 months old and very soon afterward started talking. At age 7 months, he constructed his first sentence, 'I want a nail.' He said this particular phrase after noticing a nail stuck in the wall. Most notably, his intellectual abilities surpassed his physical ones.

"How did those abilities manifest themselves?

"When Boris was just 1 year old, I started giving him letters (based on the Nikitin's system). And guess what? He was able to read large newspaper print. It didn't take long for him to get acquainted with colors and their shades. He began to paint at 2 years old. Then, soon after he turned 2, we took him to the children daycare center. Teachers were all stunned by his talents and his unusual way of thinking. The boy possesses exceptional memory and an unbelievable ability to grasp new information. However, his parents soon noticed that their child had been acquiring information in his own unique way from someplace else."

"No one has ever taught him that," recalls Nadya. "But sometimes, he would sit in a lotus position and start all these talks. He would talk about Mars, about planetary systems, distant civilizations...we couldn't believe our own ears. How can a kid know all this? Cosmos, never-ending stories of other worlds, and the immense skies are all daily mantras for him since he was 2."It was then that Boriska told us about his previous life on Mars, about the fact that the planet was, in fact, inhabited, but as a result of a powerful and destructive catastrophe, it had lost its atmosphere; nowadays all its inhabitants have to live in underground cities. Back then, he used to fly to Earth quite often for trade and other research purposes. It seems that Boriska piloted his spaceship himself. This was during the times of the Lemurian civilizations. He had a Lemurian friend who had been killed right before his own eyes."

A major catastrophe took place on Earth. A gigantic continent was consumed by stormy waters. Then suddenly, a massive rock fell on a construction...my friend was there," tells Boriska.

"I could not save him. We are destined to meet sometime in this life."

The boy envisions the entire picture of the fall of Lemuria as though it happened yesterday. He grieves the death of his best friend as though it was his fault.

One day, he noticed a book in his mother's bag entitled *Where Do We Come From?* by Ernst Muldashev. One should have seen the kind of happiness and fascination this discovery triggered in the little boy. He's been flipping through pages for hours, looking at sketches of Lemurians, photos of Tibet. He then started talking about the high intellect of the Lemurians. But Lemuria ceased to exist a minimum of 800,000 years ago. Lemurians were 9 meters tall! Is that so? How can you remember all this?"

I do remember," replied the boy. Later, he began recalling another book by Muldashev entitled *In Search of the City of Gods*. The book is mainly devoted to ancient tombs and pyramids. Boriska firmly stated that people will find knowledge under one of the pyramids (not the pyramid of Cheops). It hasn't been discovered yet.

"Life will change once the Sphinx will be opened," said he, and added that the Great Sphinx has an opening mechanism somewhere behind his ear (but he does not remember where exactly). The boy also talks with great passion and enthusiasm about the Mayan civilization. According to him, we know very little about this great civilization and its people. Most interestingly, Boriska thinks that nowadays the time has finally come for the "special ones" to be born on Earth. Planet's rebirth is approaching. New knowledge will be in great demand, a different mentality of Earthlings.

How do you know about these gifted kids and why this is happening? Are you aware that they are called "indigo" kids?

"I know that they are being born. However, I haven't met anyone in my town yet. Perhaps maybe this one girl named Yulia Petrova. She is the only one who believes me. Others simply laugh at my stories. Something is going to happen on Earth; that is why these kids are of importance. They will be able to help people. The Poles will shift. The first major catastrophe with one of the continents will happen in 2009.

Next one will take place in 2013; it will be even more devastating."

Aren't you scared that your life may also end as a result of that catastrophe?

"No. I'm not afraid. I have lived through one catastrophe on Mars already. There are still people like us out there. But after the nuclear war, everything has burnt down. Some of those people managed to survive. They built shelters and new weaponry. There was also a shift of continents there, although the continent was not as large. Martians breathe gas. In case they arrived to our planet, they would have been all standing next to pipes and breathing in fumes."

Do you prefer breathing oxygen?

"Once you are in this body, you have to breathe oxygen. However, Martians dislike this air, Earth's air, because it causes aging. Martians are all relatively young, about 30–35 years old. The amount of such Martian children will increase annually."

Boriska, why do our space stations crash before they reach Mars?

"Mars transmits special signals aimed at destroying them. Those stations contain harmful radiation."

I was amazed by his knowledge of this sort of radiation "Fobos."

This is absolutely true. Back in 1988, a resident of Volzhsky, Yuri Lushnichenko, a man with extrasensory powers, attempted to warn Soviet leaders about the inevitable crash of the first Soviet space stations Fobos-1 and Fobos-2. He also mentioned this sort of "unfamiliar" and harmful planet radiation. Obviously, no one believed him then.

What do you know about multiple dimensions? Do you know that one must fly not on straight trajectories, but maneuvering through the multidimensional space?

Boriska immediately rose to his feet and started to pour all the facts about UFOs.

"We took off and landed on Earth almost momentarily!"

The boy takes a chalk and begins drawing an oval object on a blackboard.

"It consists of six layers," he says. "Twenty-five percent outer layer, made of durable metal, 30 percent second layer made of something similar to rubber, the third layer comprises 30 percent metal. The final 4 percent is composed of a special magnetic layer. If we are to charge this magnetic layer with energy, those machines will be able to fly anywhere in the Universe."

Does Boriska have a special mission to fulfill? Is he aware of it? I pose these questions to his parents and the boy himself.

"He says he can guess," says his mother. "He says he knows something about the future of Earth. He says information will play the most significant role in the future."

Boris, how do you know all this?

"It is inside of me."

Boris, tell us why people get sick.

"Sickness comes from people's inability to live properly and be happy. You must wait for you cosmic half. One should never get involved and mess up other people's destinies. People should not suffer because of their past mistakes, but get in touch with what's been predestined for them and try to reach those heights and move on to conquer their dreams.

"You have to be more sympathetic and warm-hearted. In case someone strikes you, hug your enemy, apologize for yourself, and kneel before him. In case someone hates you, love him with all your love and devotion and ask for forgiveness. These are the rules of love and humbleness. Do you know why the Lemurians died? I am also partially at blame. They did not wish to develop spiritually any more. They went astray from the predestined path, thus destructing the overall wholeness of the planet. The Magic's Path leads to a dead end. Love is a True Magic!"

How do you know all this???

"I know...Kailis..."

What did you say?

"I said hello! This is the language of my planet."

—Gennady Belimov "NGN" Boriska is obviously a Star Child. As you read the following stories, it becomes apparent who the Star Children are. In fact, each of the groups of children will be identifiable by what they have remembered. These trends are part of why the kids are so easy to identify, although there are often overlaps of traits amongst the different groups.

Here are the set of questions that I posed to each child.

Q: **What is it like to come into this life? Is it really a choice? Do you remember when you decided to come? What was that like? Do you remember**

where you came from? Other lives you have had, or even the source of all life?

And here is what they had to say:

Grandma Chandra: It was very difficult because I knew that I would be disabled.

Q: Was it really a choice?

Grandma Chandra: Yes, it was a choice for me. I knew that I had to do "the Work."

Q: Do you remember *when* you decided to come?

Grandma Chandra: Yes, I decided when my mother and I were on Maldek before it was destroyed and became an asteroid belt.

Q: What was that like?

Grandma Chandra: It was still very difficult because I knew that I couldn't use my 3-D body. I stayed around my mother and father for 10 years before I decided to come in (be born) because I knew that my father would die, and I would be raised by my mother alone.

Q: Do you remember where you came from? Your source?

Grandma Chandra: Yes, but I cannot tell that to anyone.

Q: What about other lives you have had?

Grandma Chandra: We all have had millions of lives. The most recent Earth life for me was Lemuria.

Q: Do you remember the Source of Life?

Grandma Chandra: Yes, I remember coming from the Source of All Life.

Q: How about you, Jude?

Jude: Hard! That is the first word that came to my mind. I look around me and I see people getting plastic surgery and what not, and that does not ring true with my soul about why we are here. There is so much materialism in this world and that is not the meaning and reason that we are here.

There are times when I look out at the surroundings and I see people driving by. I think to myself all these people—everyone has a family and everyone has a place to go. Everyone is moving so fast and not seeing what is right in front of their eyes.

I see that we are destroying the Earth and the Mother that we live on, and then I think about what I can do to make this a better place. That is where the hard part comes in. It is so hard to get a message across even with the mass media being a plethora of avenues to tell a message. It is hard to be recognized among the masses when you have a truth to tell. It is hard.

Q: Do you remember that coming here was a choice?

Jude: Honestly, I know that it is a choice to come here and to come back over and over again. I see it like a line of souls waiting in a space to become human. There are so many that are lined up and willing to come here, even though there are billions of people here already.

I do not remember the choice to come back here, although I am seeing more and more each day the reason why I did chose to come back. In search of answers, I contacted an internationally known mystic. She helped me realize that I choose to come back. In a recent reading she told me that my soul was ancient, before Earth, and that I chose to come back here to relay an intergalactic message to the masses. That was the confirmation that I needed to hear because I knew this from the beginning.

There was an incident that jogged my soul. This incident happened when I was 19 years old, and it was an out-of-body experience. I died and came back. It was after this experience that I knew that I chose to come here when I was born and chose to come back from death. There was a reason for me to exist. I just had to find that reason with every breath I took from then on.

Q: What about the Source, where you came from in the beginning, do you remember?

Jude: I know that my soul energy did not come from the Earth plane. I have recently been searching for where my soul energy originated. I know the obvious origination point in the thoughts of the Creator; however, I know that there is more to it than I can fully understand at this point.

The place my soul energy came from was there before Earth and even this solar system. That is all I know at this time, although I have and will continue to search until I know. From the moment I came back into this life after my death experience I began to unravel the long cord of my soul's journeys. I also gained the perspective of the ultimate paradoxes of life. The major one being time and space.

Q: How about past lives? What's your take on that?

Jude: I know now that all past lives are happening at the same time in slightly lower or higher frequency dimensions. They resemble this Earth that is NOW, however they are continually growing in their own time and no time at all, hence the paradox. Upon that comprehension I realized that I could use the abilities and talents from my past lives and future lives in the NOW. It was then that I truly began the awakening and realignment of my soul and life purpose in my present incarnation.

Q: What about you, Weston? Tell us about your experience in coming here.

Weston: I was happy to come. Once I arrived on Earth I realized that I didn't always have to stay put, that I could leave my body anytime that I wanted, so I travel outside of myself a lot. That makes being human more bearable. Consciousness is an infinite field of energy and having to keep it inside of a human body all of the time wouldn't be fun at all. I am very sensitive when I am in my body because my energy is so big. Because of this I don't like to wear clothes or shoes.

Q: Have you had other lives? Can you remember?

Weston: I have had a multitude of lives, most of them intergalactic. I still hang out with my friends "out there." Sometimes they even come with me close to the Earth plane and we visit other people who can see us.

Q: Was there one life that stands out above the others?

Weston: My most prominent experience was in Atlantis where I played a very important role in maintaining the balance within the crystalline grid. Our entire grid system was based on what you now call the ley lines of the Earth. We could build energy for power and we could direct the energy anywhere we wanted. It was in this way that we maintained balance on the planet. Our energy fields also affected the weather. We could predict and change the weather based on activity in the grid. This energy field was a living organism just like all other life. It sustained itself based on the needs of the Earth, balancing, equalizing, and keeping things like earthquakes to a minimum. There are places on the Earth where there are great big releases of energy. This energy is electromagnetic just like human consciousness. Because of this we were able to intuitively stay in touch with the Earth and its life along with ours. It was a mutual situation.

There were other people in Atlantis who found that the power we had harnessed could be utilized for selfish reasons, to make weapons to hurt other people, and to create an imbalance in the grid so that some people had everything and others got nothing.

Because of that, I removed a particular crystalline key that was vital to the operation of the power grid. Without that, no one could change the balance or the direction of the energy field. Ultimately, a man named Lian was able to restore the grid to full power. In his earnest to become more powerful than anyone else, he initiated a coup. There was a battle in the main generator vault and one of the main enhancers was knocked out of harmony with the others. The magnetic field was knocked awry. This created instability in the Earth grid, which ultimately led to huge seismic activity and the demise of our civilization. Many of us were away on expeditions and survived the tumult. Some of us went to what is now called Polynesia. Others went to what is now the frozen South Pole. It wasn't frozen then. Some of us landed in what is now Egypt. At first, in ancient Egypt the people there were primitive, but we showed them some of our technologies and they began to flourish. Unfortunately greed was again present, and the technologies became mysteries to most, and known to only a few who used the mysteries to control other people. Through time the technologies were diluted by the telling, and we became worshiped as deities instead of the loving people that we were.

I have had other lives too, but the most important thing is the life I have right now. What was, was.

Q: What about your Source, Weston? Where you came from in the very beginning?

Weston: Sure, I remember the Source. I still go there sometimes, when I feel like I need to be evened out. It is one great field of light and energy where you are everything and nothing all at the same time. There is no singular feeling, only bliss. You are aware of everything all at once—all-knowing—and at the same time, still aware of self. This light field is the point of beginning for all life-forms and realities. It is also where all life-forms will ultimately return.

Q: Tristan, what do you remember about coming to Earth this time?

Tristan: I didn't want to come to Earth because I remembered a lot of my past lives that weren't good at all. God and I talked (in our minds) for a long time. I told God that I didn't want to come here because I didn't want to experience so much pain and sadness again. God told me that it was important for me to come back to Earth because I needed to teach people how to love again since so many had forgotten.

Q: What do you remember about choosing your family?

Tristan: I remember being with God, Jesus, and my Spirit Guides, selecting my Earth parents. We picked out my mom and dad, and I was told that they would take good care of me. I traveled through a very large, dark tube when I came to Earth.

(Christina remembers being in her light body as she went through the Book of Life, choosing her journey.)

Christina: What I really remember is being in a large space with what seemed like clouds in bright pink, orange-like colors, and there was a book that I could flip through to choose what life I wanted to live.

Q: Were you in physical form or something else?

Christina: I didn't feel like I had a physical body, but I was floating. After I was done looking I don't remember what happened after that.

Q: Is there some process or practice that helps you remember?

Christina: When I meditate I can explore and remember more.

Rhianna: Coming into life is a choice. I remember when I decided to come.... I went to a huge purple portal, and I saw myself in my mom's stomach; three days later I was born. This life is easier; before I was a princess with a little horse. Now, I don't have to take pony lessons, I don't have to live in a palace, and I don't have knights surrounding me all the time. And those shoes I had to wear really hurt my feet!

(Nathan remembers what many call the Crystal City. There, everything, even the atmosphere, has a silvery, reflective nature. Beyond our third dimension, many of the beings are very tall compared to human beings. It is details like this that tell me the memories are authentic!)

Nathan: I remember when I decided to come to life again. My soul picked Mommy and Daddy and even my sister. Heaven was a huge place! I had a silver home with silver stairs. I was happy. All my friends were big like my dad.

Q: Do you remember anything about the life you had before this one?

Nathan: I remember once there were a bunch of bad guys and I fighted (sic) them. My home got destroyed. There was this trap in my house you could get lost in and there wasn't any food.

Q: How about you, Jasin? What do you remember?

(Jasin talks about what it is to become limited, to inhabit a human body....)

Jasin: It is hard because you have to fit into this tiny space.

Q: Do you remember other times you lived?

Jasin: I came from Luvezorite. It is two galaxies away. Its color is turquoise. The Luvs live there and come visit us to make sure our air is okay. I remember being here before as a velociraptor. I was friends with a T. Rex then. I was a fish before that. I have also been a grey wolf. I was a sculptor named Rodin before.

Q: Was there anyone there that is in your life now?

Jasin: Grandma GG was my baby then, but she didn't live that long. I was also a man named John Luther.

Q: What was going on at that time?

Jasin: There were lots of wars then. I did not like that. People still rode horses then. When the Spaniards came to America, there were lots of wars. That time I just died from getting old.

Q: Joseph, do you remember anything specific?

Joseph: It's very complicated. I don't know what other planets I could have been born on, how peaceful or what they are like. Life out there is possible. I'm just here because they put me here rather than somewhere else. I can't say or compare it to anything, so I don't know how to answer this.

Q: Is it really a choice?

Joseph: It could be a choice. I like it here. I like my friends and everyone else here. I think it could be a better planet, that's for sure. I think that we could do a lot more with this planet. I think that we are a lot wasteful but I think that it may have been a choice. I may want to help this planet but I don't know.

Q: Do you remember where you came from? Other lives you have had, or even the Source of all life?

(Joseph refers to vague memories of his past lives. These memories often fade as the children reach age 6 or 7, but not always.)

Joseph: No, I don't know, but there are some things that I envision real good, that I have not seen. I think that it could be a tiny speck of memory. I mean that other lives are probably long, maybe longer than I have lived, though I may have just hit the surface of what I could have seen. So I think that I kind of.... Sometimes I have a really good gut feeling that tells me that's what it's like. I don't think I have ever seen or felt whatever I have. I don't think that they were on this planet because I can envision a really good Black Hole. Obviously I have never been to one.

Q: What about you, Scott?

Scott: Yes. I came from the island of Montanui. It's at the end of this dimension. You have to travel 125 septillion miles to what the Earth people call "west." I remember living on Montanui and what kept us alive.

Q: What was that like?

Scott: The people on Montanui were mechanical-like beings, but they had feelings just like humans, only instead of blood, they had a strange substance that flows in them called "protodermis." The way you would tell if they were alive or sleeping, is that there is a little light around your heart that glows when you are alive and out when you are dead.

Q: Were you ever on Earth before?

Scott: I remember two past lives on Earth. One is Cleopatra and the other is Robin Hood. Then I know a past life on the island of Voyganui, but I don't know how to describe its shape. It's kinda like a stretched out crescent, only one end is longer. And I was Toah-Jovan at the time, the Toah of Magnetism.

Q: Ahn, what do you recall about coming to this life, or times before this?

Ahn: Coming to this life is very frustrating, interesting, beautiful, and physically limited.

Q: Is it a choice?

Ahn: Definitely it is a choice. Actually, everything is a choice.

Q: Where did you come from?

Ahn: I told my mother when I was 10 years old that I wanted to be just a blob floating in the air with intense love; I feel that's where I came from.

Q: What else do you remember?

Ahn: I know I also came from Andromeda; I had a very important life there. I have drawn pictures of my big sister and other souls I knew there. Other past lives that I remember are as an Egyptian in ancient Egypt and also as a native Indian who talked with trees. I left some messages for myself for the future, so I will have to talk to some trees sometime soon.

(Gabriel doesn't quite remember.)

Gabriel: I am sure it was a choice and it must have been amazing.

Q: Scotty, do you have a sense that you have been here before? Do you remember any of your past lives? Big memories or even little flashes?

Scotty: Most definitely. The biggest one for me was when I was little I was obsessed with the Titanic, and I was so scared of big boats and huge ships. I would be the one to sleep in the lifeboat. Just the idea of being trapped under all that steel with all of those things flying around you. I really believe that I was on the Titanic. That has always been a major issue for me.

When I see ivory pillars or the big redwood trees, it definitely takes me back to what I call the olden times, where everything was soul-based and so much simpler than it is now. Especially when I am in a forest, I am totally at one with everything.

Q: You had some memories about Egypt too, didn't you?

Scotty: Yeah, I totally want to go to Egypt and see everything again because I was a very influential figure there. I think I was the high priest in one of the main temples or in the temple of the cats, because I am so connected to cats. I have a cat, and whenever she is sitting by me it takes me back to being in the temple with all the cats. They were so sacred, and if you killed a cat you were condemned to hanging; they were such sacred animals back then.

And also, when I smell bay leaves, I think that I was at Delphi....

Q: Really?

Scotty: Yes, because when I smell bay leaves I get really activated. I need to hear the ocean and go underground. I definitely think that if I smelled sulfur and bay leaves at the same time, that would be so intense because I would just go back there.

Q: You would just zone out?

Scotty: Yeah, It would be so intense.

Q: Lindsay, for you, was coming to Earth a choice?

Lindsay: I completely believe it was a choice. I think it's a bit hard to remember when I decided to come. My previous life was interrupted rather abruptly, so I came back within 20 years of my last life.

Q: Do you remember anything about making the choice or choosing your parents?

Lindsay: I had a dream once when I was younger, around 7 years old. I was sitting around a table with some figures; at the time I was not sure who they all were. We were discussing an entry of some sort and they were saying that there were still a few choices I had to make. That was all I remember, but I had a feeling when I woke up, which made me believe that incident had actually happened.

Q: Do you remember where you came from? Other lives you have had, or even the Source of all life?

Lindsay: When I was 5 years old, I decided I wanted to be named Scott. I was determined not to answer to any other name. That went on for about three months.

Later when I had a past-life regression done I brought up that information, and as it turns out that was my name from my last life. As my mother can tell you, I was a tomboy growing up, and my favorite games to play with the other kids always involved soldiers or fighters. I discover later that the reason I felt so attached to the military was because I was in Vietnam, and was shot and killed during my second tour.

Funny how I then chose a father who also served two tours in Vietnam. The Source of life as I see it is warm and bright. It is not really an entity, yet it is all the same. We are part of it just as much as it is a part of us. It's hard to really explain because the source is more a feeling of oneness and love than an actual being.

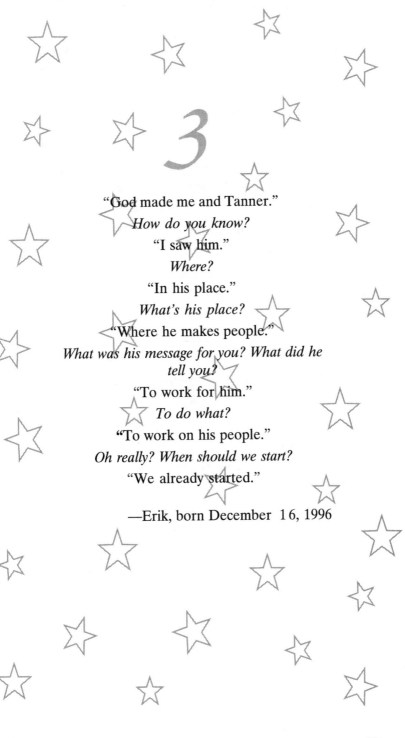

3

"God made me and Tanner."

How do you know?

"I saw him."

Where?

"In his place."

What's his place?

"Where he makes people."

What was his message for you? What did he tell you?

"To work for him."

To do what?

"To work on his people."

Oh really? When should we start?

"We already started."

—Erik, born December 16, 1996

THE SOUL'S JOURNEY
BY JUDE DECOFF
(© JUDE DECOFF, 2007)

All who read this listen to your Soul
Now you have the power and ability to grow
You are not alone there are hundreds around
You search and search yet answers unfound
You will not use your eyes to see the truth
Instead you will use your heart connecting to youth
The children born NOW are connected
Special souls with much intended
Listen to them and combine their message with yours
As the power and truth grows into a double-edged sword
Justice judges what is right or wrong
Leaders lead without a song
A passion, A light, A spark within
We all hold the power to create and begin
Begin the journey to your reality
You see things from your eyes but you only do see
Each person soon will create their own world
Much of what is taught comes in energy swirls
It rises and falls with intent it creases
Pauses and stops and then it ceases
It merges with your purpose and power
Then creates your reality as a beautiful flower.

I Am...

W ho are we in relation to everyone and everything else? Do we even know? What gifts have we brought to our planet that perhaps we have lost sight of or forgotten completely?

As we are born into our human lives, each of us carries a specific energy that is uniquely ours. In fact, our personal combinations of harmonics are unique in all of creation; there is no one else who is exactly like us. The energies are literally sets of harmonic frequencies. You might think of each person as infinite musical chords, a virtual symphony of energies. Each of those symphonies *is* us; and on deep, deep levels, each of us knows that inherently, but we aren't aware. We just don't consciously remember.

Our energy sets not only identify us, they carry information for us as well. The entire road map of our being is contained in our energy sets. At the same time, the energies communicate with all of creation, telling the infinite every detail about our experiences. Concurrently, our energy fields are also receiving information that brings guidance to us, if we are listening. In other words, what we do in every moment that we exist is communicated infinitely outward; and at the same time, we inwardly receive endless information that can help us make informed choices in our lives. In every given moment, we are an integral part of creation, and we contribute to the reality of the whole. This makes us powerful creators in our own right.

In addition to our identities and our communicative abilities, our energy sets also dictate the types of abilities and awareness we have in this life. What I mean is, the way our energy systems are arranged, and the frequencies at which they vibrate, determine our giftedness in many ways. One of those gifts is how aware we are outside of third-dimensional reality. Others might be, but are not limited to, our psychic capabilities, telepathic abilities, or the ability to see beings other than those in this reality. These are just some of the things that people call "gifts." There are others, of course; for example, something as simple as being observant of others, and knowing how they feel or what they really mean. The possibilities of giftedness amongst human beings is as unlimited as our imaginations.

When we are born, we have awareness of our integral belonging. We can see and feel energy. Sometimes we are still in contact with the place from which we just came. We don't yet have an identity of being individual; we learn that. People talk to us as if we are unintelligent. They teach us to be afraid. They teach us perceptions of "our place" amongst other humans. As a result, we lose our sense of the infinite and become limited in conscious awareness. The doors to our infinite awareness close.

As we become more mature, having good life experience and perceptions of responsibility, we begin to take ourselves way too seriously. *Life* becomes too serious. We forget the innocence of who we are and of what we are capable. We forget the awareness that we have an infinitely choreographed database of information that is available to us. As children we still have that awareness, but soon our thinking minds take over.

We use our thinking minds to rationalize everything, and that doesn't always serve us to our greatest potential. Our thinking minds actually close the doors to greater reality. When we use our logical minds, our higher awareness literally gets locked out, and our brain waves shift to lower vibrations.

I wondered if the children would or could tell me what energies they bring to our Earth. Their answers told me that their senses of identity were similar to each other, but also had far-reaching differences. Their clarity was astounding.

The question presented to each child was this:

Q: **What kind of energy do you bring to our Earth? What do you represent and why are you here? In other words, who is (child's name)? Why aren't all children like you?**

Grandma Chandra: I bring the knowledge and the energies of Lemuria and Atlantis.

Q: Who is Grandma Chandra??

Grandma Chandra: Grandma Chandra is an Omni-Dimensional Being who has come here to awaken the planet and put people on the road to ascension. I have many forms. Some are dolphin, whale, bird, beautiful woman.

Q: How come all children aren't like you?

Grandma Chandra: It is not in their contracts. All of us have a contract or contracts. Each one has their own "job."

Jude: The energy that I bring is far out. That is the only way that I can describe it without knowing exactly how far out. I know that I have been every organism on this Earth, and that I was here prior to the Earth and our solar system's creation. The energy that I bring is very high vibration.

I supposedly have "ADD"! However the way I see it is that ADD is actually the evolution of the human mind. It is comparable to computer motherboards. There are new motherboards that are out that use the system known as hyper-pipelining. In common language that is the ability for the computer to send information to where it needs to go at hyper-speeds.

What do doctors and the general public say about children that are classified with ADD? That we are hyper and move too fast! The human mind is evolving just as our souls and Earth are evolving. ADD as I have been shown is the "in between" of the next form of the human brain. The reason that we are able to multitask as we do is because we are using far more than 10 percent of our brain capacity.

The ADD or hyper-brain stimulation is providing us with different access points and a far greater expanse to utilize our brain, and ultimately this body, to a higher level than ever has been accomplished before.

The energy that I bring comes in the form of communication.

Q: Can you give us some examples of this?

Jude: I am able to visualize and effectively communicate positive visualizations that anyone can understand. I know answers to questions that people have before they ask me the question.

Another example would be the World Puja Web radio show. The topics that the guests talk about with Dr. Meg and Maureen are topics that I have already been discussing with my Indigo family who live across the world and United States three months prior. I move much faster than most people. In that fast frequency, vibrations, and movement I am able to tap into the future. I do not get visions per say, rather my thoughts come from future incidents and times. It is knowledge that I have learned already; however, time has not caught up to me. When I receive the confirmations and synchronicities, that is when I know that time has caught up with me.

For now it seems that three months is the time, as topics that are validation and confirmation for me come into my earthly experiences about three months after I have discussed them and moved on to new thoughts. I don't know what to call my type of energy, but it is somewhere in between here and there. I sense and feel that I represent change. I represent mobility. I represent cross-cultural and dimensional communication. I represent humanity.

Q: Why would you say that all kids aren't like you?

Jude: To say that other children or young adults are not like me is an understatement and a paradox, as I am aware that we are all individuals, yet we are all one. It is from within that oneness that the individual was formed, and that we received our facet to call our soul's reality.

My reality is very different than anyone else's other than Creator's, as I am living through His reality; however, the only reasons are the experiences that I have had in this life. I have lived many lives in this one life. I have held many different jobs; I have been homeless for a short time; I have been the entertainer; I have been the homemaker; I have been the young, the old, and the new; I have been the companion for survival purposes; and I have died and returned to breathe in this life. Living multiple lives in this one is the major access point of my energy and my abilities.

Q: What do you mean?

Jude: I have experienced so much, and that is where I obtain my connection and power from the Creator—I am as much the Creator as the Creator is myself and everyone on the planet and beyond. It is through these experiences that I gained approval of lessons completed. It is only through life experiences that I have evolved and grown into who I am NOW. I am no different from other children than they are different from me. I have just had separate and different experiences that someday they may have as well.

I am writing a biography that tells more about the individual experiences that I have had, as there have been hundreds in my 25 years. It is these experiences that make us who we are, and ultimately human expressions of creation.

Q: Weston, what kind of energy do you bring to us through your experience?

Weston: I bring the notion of the impossible to light. What I mean is that I have come to show people that there is more to reality than they think. By communicating with people telepathically and creating awareness of possibilities beyond simple human senses, I am helping people remember who they are beyond the restrictions of "human being." After all, I have a physical body that doesn't work very well, but then my consciousness is unlimited. It is a lot of fun for me to see the surprise in people's hearts and on their faces when I show up unannounced in their awareness.

Q: You can do that?

Weston: Sure, as easily as you breathe. I can project my consciousness anywhere that I want.

Q: I know that you are a really talented guy. Let's talk about what else you bring to our world.

Weston: I also give people faith in their giftedness, because when they discover that they can communicate with me telepathically and ethereally, they know beyond a doubt that there is plenty to believe in, plenty to trust.

Another part of the energy I bring to Earth is of mischief and innocence. Really, having a sense of humor helps! If people can't laugh at me or at themselves they are going to have a hard time.

The other element of why I am here is to show people that just because the physical body may not work right doesn't mean that a person is any less. By being able to do the things that I do, contacting people telepathically and being instrumental in things happening, all of which is verifiable because I make sure to give several people the same or similar information, I am a perfect example that there is much more to life than how people look or what their bodies can do.

Q: So that's why you do it! I am beginning to understand just how brilliant you really are! So tell me, Weston, why aren't other children like you?

Weston: All children aren't like me because it would be too much of a reality shift for people. I don't think they could handle it.

(Well that was honest!)

Q: So Tristan, Peter, what about you?

Tristan: My energy is very light and loving. I don't know why other children are not like me. Maybe they watch too much TV.

Peter: My energy is a Creator's energy that wants to fix all things in life.

Q: Christina, what is your sense of what you bring to Earth?

Christina: I think I am someone who chose this life to raise others' vibrations so that they can pass it on. I also think that I am supposed to work with children. I think other children aren't like us because they showed some signs (that they were special) and their parents told them it was bad or punished them because they thought they were possessed, and they learned to push that part of them away.

Rhianna: I bring high energy to the world! I came here to start a new life, to learn about technology, and to have fun! Other children aren't like me because I have a different aura.

(Jasin had a more holistic approach to his answers...)

Jasin: I'm not going to answer that.

Q: Why?

Jasin: We are *all one*. Everybody is me, so why answer that question? I bring all sorts of energy and so do you.

(And a great point at that! Gotta love Jasin's direct approach!)

Q: Joseph, what about you?

Joseph: Conflict resolution, peace; in other words, peaceful, joyful. I stand for truth, and I think that I'm here to stop conflict and other struggles trying to bring peace. I would like to be here for that. I don't know much more than that.

Q: Why isn't everyone like you?

Joseph: They may have a different purpose. This may not be their purpose. Maybe they just don't want to see it, so they reject this kind of purpose. No two people are alike.

Q: Scott?

Scott: I represent a being of just true happiness, though at times I can get angry. I'm here to find out where all the chaos is coming from.

(And then Scott addresses free will...)

Q: Why are you different from others?

Scott: Because, all children are able to have their own opinion and their own beliefs. All children have the right to have their own unique opinions and beliefs, which leads to different behaviors and different energies being put out.

Ahn: The energy that I bring to Earth is blue energy—acceptance of everything that is—and joy from the soul. Who am I? Who I am is many things. We are all connected, so I am everything and nothing.

Q: Ahn, why do you think all children aren't like you?

Ahn: All children are not like me because I chose to "wake up" early consciously. I notice whenever I'm in my teenage ego and I prefer being in my higher self. I am extremely sensitive to energies. I also cry if I ever tell a lie, and I have many out-of-this-world experiences.

Q: What do you represent on our Earth?

Ahn: I feel I represent being in truth, and I'm here to be an example of speaking and living that truth. I have to write—something just drives me from inside, and my poetry and lyrics seem to touch people, so I believe this is what I came here to do.

Q: Recently you changed your name? Why?

Ahn: Jasmine is my given name, and in the last year I have discovered other names of mine, soul names I believe, and they are Ahn and Zinda (A to Z; the beginning and the end). I use Ahn more than Jasmine now—but it can get confusing for people when you change names. I was stuttering over "Jasmine," and told my mother I just wanted to have something simple such as "Ahn."

Q: Hi Scotty! What have you come to the Earth to do?

Scotty: I personally think that I am in this world to change this world. To change, to challenge...all of that. I was most disturbed when I was talking with the head of my school because I was asking, "what is the point?" Like I am never going to use any of this. I asked him if he remembered everything that *he* had learned in algebra and he was like, "No." And I said, "Okay," and I came to this realization that children in our society aren't asking why.

The people who are getting by aren't asking why. And I was really affected by this because from kindergarten, people are supposed to teach you to ask why, always ask why, *always ask questions*, and that the people who aren't are the ones who are succeeding in this society. I was really contemplating that and I thought, wow, I really want to ask why and I'm getting shut down for asking why.

Q: Because you are considered insolent and insubordinate?

Scotty: Because I am defying normal procedures.

Q: And you aren't staying "in the box." You want to know more and they don't want to tell you?

Scotty: Right.

Q: Well maybe they really don't know....

Scotty: Right, and what if I don't want to write my essays with an outline, and then I am told, "well that is how it has always been done." Hasn't culture always been changing? Am I one of those people who are changing our culture? Who are breaking out of those paradigms? What if we still wrote in medieval style? What if no one ever changed that?

Q: And if we still lived and spoke in that cultural way...

Scotty: Right—in the way of the dark, of segregation and all of that.

Q: It would only be about survival then. It wouldn't be about evolving full circle...

Scotty: I totally agree.

Q: Gabriel?

Gabriel: I represent kindness and equality. I am here to help mankind. I want to change that people fight all of the time and do not really know each other.

Q: Why do you think that is?

Gabriel: Maybe because they believe everything they see. People cannot see their truth anymore because things such as video games and TV hide the truth.

Q: Why do you think you can see through this when so many others can't or don't?

Gabriel: I think I can see through because I have been here so many times, and last time I realized that what we are told is not always the truth. I do not have any more or less reason to be here than anyone else. I am not special; I would just gladly help the world see more clearly. I just feel like if you are kind to people they will want inside of them to be kind back.

Q: How does it feel, being how you are?

Gabriel: It feels good that I have this peacefulness inside of me. I think God gave me this peacefulness so others can remember they want this too.

Q: Why do you think you are like this?

Gabriel: I am not sure why I am like this. Maybe it happened at the time I was born.

Q: Lindsay, I have known you for a long time and know that you are a wonderful, gifted being. Who would you say is Lindsay?

Lindsay: Who is Lindsay? I am not too sure that is possible to put into words. I remember back in elementary school they would ask you to describe yourself in three words. I once raised my hand and told the teacher that I couldn't do that, because "there aren't any right words." I still believe that to this day, but for the purposes of this book and this interview I will put it like this: I am me and all of the above. I am too many things to name, yet the two-letter word *me* seems to fit. Its something you can't explain. You can try to put yourself in categories such as caring, kind, funny, and smart. But in the end everyone has a little bit of each of those things...that's where the "all of the above" comes in.

I have been given certain gifts that some children have not fully developed, but again we are all one, and we are different, yet the same. I am sorry to be so cliché, but it is the truth.

4

You have to have all types of experiences, spirit and human, to be complete.

—Lindsay

The PURPOSE *of* LIFE: WHY WE ARE HERE

It seems to me that everyone is looking for their one single reason for being on Earth. In fact, the question that I am most often asked is, "What is my purpose?"

I have come to the conclusion that this is a generational issue. In previous generations, we were told that we have to do *better*, be *more*, study *harder*, and so on, and yet, *rarely*, if *ever* did *anyone* tell us that we had done a great job, only that we could *do better next time*.

It was kind of like being given a destination without a road map. The result of that has been countless adults with poor self-esteem who have yet to recognize their giftedness and who constantly search for how to fix themselves.

For many of us, finding our way through life has been difficult. Because we aren't in touch with our own inner truth, we often don't know how to feel or why we feel out of sync with everyone else. We often have low self-esteem because we haven't a clue about where we are going, or even where we have been for that matter. That is because we are measuring our lives by the values and expectations of others. WE are still tying to please our parents, teachers, and others who were the authority figures in our childhoods. Often we will attract others who will continue to challenge us in similar ways until we learn that we have our own journey to travel, and it doesn't look anything like the one we have been on!

Because of these understandings, I have come to the conclusion that our purpose is not singular, but to be found in every moment that we exist. Because we truly are part of everything and everything *is* us, we are continually interrelating on a universal scale. From the tiniest expression of energy to any intentional act, we affect everything in and around us, and we never know just how much we do.

My favorite story is one of a miracle in a moment, from my friend whom we'll call Barbara:

"I was standing in line at the post office, contemplating suicide. My husband had died unexpectedly and I felt devastated, completely alone in the world. I felt as if I had nothing. I was beyond depressed. I felt as if I had no reason to live. I was unloved and unwanted. There was nothing left, so I was going to go home and kill myself.

As the lines began to move, the lady in the line adjacent to me turned to me and smiled. Just smiled. In that tiny moment I felt acknowledged, alive. I decided that life wasn't so bad after all. That woman will never know that her small act of kindness saved my life that day...."

Of course all of our actions beget reactions. In fact, every cause has an effect. This is called "ripple effect." What has this beautiful soul done with the life that was saved by a simple smile? She moved to a small village in another country where she teaches the natives how to support their families through farming and learning crafts such as jewelry making. She also works at a school, teaching the children different crafts that they can use to support themselves and their families in the future.

All from one smile.

The Children of Now recognize the beauty of the moment. They are also aware that they have come to Earth with a grand purpose. For most of them that purpose is to teach us how to love each other, because we seem to have forgotten. But their purposes don't stop there.

I wanted to take this subject as deep as the children were willing to go, so I asked them:

Q: **What is the real purpose of human being? What is the best way to serve that purpose? Are the directions we choose in our lives important? Why are we here when we can be Spirit?**

Q: Nicholas, how about you?

Nicholas: I might as well tell you I am not an ordinary guy. What makes me extraordinary is not the fact that I am in a wheelchair, yet from an early age, I have had amazing clarity about my spiritual mission in life.

I would like to share with many that I am here to help the Earth prepare for the Earth's transition into light and love. This may sound ethereal; however, it is really coinciding with processes of creation and dissolution. We can find this evident throughout history. We are entering into a new time where our challenge is to cocreate our future while being in the NOW. This is our lesson. However, our main learning tool is more about acquiring experience and less about me teaching.

When I and the other children arrive we bring crystal energy vibration or cosmic energy vibration so that we may collectively raise the Earth's vibration. This is already happening at a phenomenal rate. Do not be alarmed by this, as it is a natural part of our evolution.

Just as dinosaurs came and went, this is another step in the Divine plan that keeps us humble.

I have known from an early age that I am here with great destiny and purpose to help others remember pure love, like in the way Jesus taught. I am to do this in unique ways, yet mostly through writing and talks.

Will you join me in feeling the Earth's vibration as it becomes lighter? In this way the Earth will receive a huge gift in the flow of love.

Jude: The purpose of being a human is to learn about emotions and the use of our five senses. There is no other sentient race that can learn about these two things in the way that humans can. True love is our quest; to learn to be an individual while also balancing the oneness with the Creator.

Humility seems to be the most productive way of achieving the learning process of these ideals and goals that we have put forth in human form. The only thing that you need to think about when making a life-changing or direction-changing choice is this: am I doing this out of pure love? If the answer is yes then you are making the right decision. This includes love for you, your family, humanity, and Earth. We are here because there is no way that we could learn these lessons in spirit. Spirit cannot emotionally connect. Spirit can not use the five senses. These are our gifts and can only be used in human form. There are so many souls that are in line to become human for this very reason. Only humans can be human. We are also here to master unity and individuality and their delicate balance. True love is the key to opening the door to the Creator, and that is felt through and practiced through living through love, and using the five senses and emotions to master the balancing of the male and female, so that we may return to the Creator complete.

Weston: We are here to experience the tangible. When we are not in our physical bodies, the feelings are so full, so complete, that it is impossible to experience them individually. At the same time, when we are in our physical bodies, we can experience emotion, thought, feelings, and other more subtle aspects of being. As we exist, as we live in that existence, we communicate our experiences back to the infinite. As we do, the Universe creates even more possibilities for us and others to experience. You see, when it comes right down to it, we are all contributing to the life experiences of each other.

Tristan: We are here to be loving to every living thing.

Christina: The real purpose of human beings is to have experiences and to learn for the greater good. There are no "good" or "bad" directions, there are only experiences to be had. The way we perceive them changes the way we experience things. When we are in spirit, we cannot have the physical exposure to things.

(Nathan has memories of his home being destroyed in his previous life, of being trapped and not being able to get out.)

Nathan: I'm here now to put my home back together.

Rhianna: The purpose of human beings is to make stuff and to experience life—to learn and have fun! Direction in life is important; we are here for God.

Jasin: We are here from our soul-selves to help Earth generate new lives of peace.

Joseph: Conflict resolution, peace; in other words, peaceful, joyful. I stand for truth and I think that I'm here to stop conflict and other struggles trying to bring peace. I would like to be here for that. I don't know much more than that.

Q: Why aren't all children like you?

Joseph: They may have a different purpose. This may not be their purpose. Maybe they just don't want to see it, so they reject this kind of purpose. No two people are alike.

Q: What is the real purpose of human being? What is the best way to serve that purpose?

Scott: I've thought of this question before, and we are here to learn, not judge.

Q: Are the directions we choose in our lives important? Why are we here when we can be Spirit?

Scott: They are.

Ahn: Taking care of our holy temple and loving it for what it is no matter what; living different experiences, seeing our mirrors, and learning with love always, if you choose. Directions we choose in this world are major and minor; minor being having fun, and major being making a positive difference in humankind. We can be in Spirit, like a blob floating in pure love, and I wish this sometimes, but it is our soul's choice to be here in the physical now.

Gabriel: To destroy the inner greed that we all have. We chose to have form and be tested. When we are all Spirit we are with God, and so it is all right there in front of us. When we are in our bodies we get to test how we can reflect back the good.

Lindsay: To love. It's really as simple as that. We are the ones that make everything so complicated. We have been Spirit. There, loving is easy, because we know nothing else. Here we have to start from scratch. We are working our way up in our bodies. Each generation comes in with more recent information and experiences to help us grow as a people. You have to have all types of experiences, spirit and human, to be complete.

5

...The really amazing thing
is that all of the information within
the universe is within us.
we could sit in a meadow our entire lives and
know everything that is going on
if we would just be willing to discover
what is in us...

—Scotty

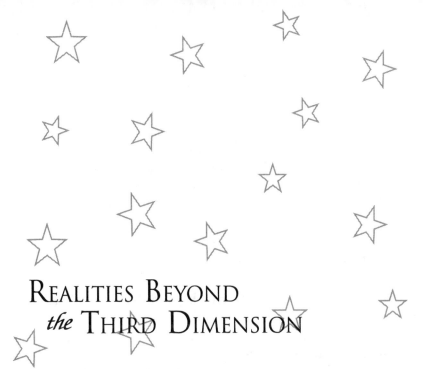

REALITIES BEYOND
the THIRD DIMENSION

The Children of Now often talk about other realities. They share stories about experiences that they have with Beings who are not of our reality. Some of those Beings are relatives or others who have transitioned to the Otherworld. The children also talk about other Beings, such as their Spirit Guides or Angels, and even others who come and go in the perceptions of the children. These stories are not made up or fantasies of the imagination.

The truth is that some of our children can literally see through the veils that separate this reality from others. Beyond that, the children are actually interactive within those realities, living in them as easily as they do in our world. Our children learn from, play with, and make friends with people whom the rest of us don't even know exist. Knowing this really gives different meaning to the idea of invisible friends!

The stories that the children tell vary from taking out-of-body trips to Atlantis, to star systems in parallel universes, and even into interactive multidimensionality. The children talk about other people that they see and with whom they interact, of Beings who are not in human form, and are not in our plane of reality. They converse with Angels and comfortably talk with their Spirit Guides as if they were you or me. To the Children of Now, these beings are as real as you and me.

I thought is would not only be fun, but a real education for us to experience some of the children's experiences within other worlds, so I asked them:

Q: Are there other worlds beyond this one? What are they like?

Grandma Chandra: Billions. Other worlds that are organized into societies. Many can't be seen, felt, or heard, and are in dimensions that we have not yet discovered.

Jude: I have always felt that my energy and soul were from another part of the Universe. As the Star Gate opened recently, I felt the energies of my soul family coming forward from the other side. I know through my gifts that they have come to aid us in our own personal transformations and ascensions. Since the energies from other parts of the Universe have entered into our world I have gained many new perspectives and enhanced my personal abilities.

There was also an occurrence when I encountered intergalactic messengers. I was meditating on the inner refractions of light within a large crystal ball. I saw a line up of sentient beings that were no doubt from other parts of the Universe; it reminded me much of the cantina scene within the *Star Wars* movies. I looked around at these beings and they were many shapes, sizes, and sexes. I saw beings that were very tall who wore brown cloaks, and short beings who had no eyes or nose, just indentations instead.

There is no doubt in my reality that there is life beyond this one planet. I see it as a one-shot deal. Creator would by no means put all of His energy into this one Earth without another plan.

I see the Earth as an interstellar "experiment." When I was 19, I saw this confirmation in a vision along with a friend. The vision indicated that we are a culmination of many different soul energies that represent different parts of the galaxy. To me, the beings on other planets are all one body type. That varies from planet to planet. They do not have the racial differences that we on Earth perceive.

This perception of differences among the human race is one of our key aspects and lessons that we are here to learn, however it also brings many issues when free will is thrown into the mix. I know, having experienced the varied races of the Earth and the singular races of the other planets that we are truly a unique planet. We seem to be held back due to the vast differences among the visual aspects of humanity as well as the combination of free will and ego.

I also had another vision that the planets in our own solar system once had life on them. This goes along with the idea that there was previous life on Mars. Where Earth once was in its current position, Mars existed. Earth was where Venus is now, and the other planets one space behind their current placements. There was another planet that was in the position that Mars is in now.

In the vision I saw that the planets feed the sun so that the sun can still exist and support life within our solar system. I saw Mars like Earth is today, and that the positioning of the planets is what creates the atmosphere that can support evolving life. However, once Mars got too close to the sun, the water evaporated and the atmosphere became stagnant and harsh.

Venus is being prepared to become the new Earth and Earth will eventually fall into the dismal space that Mars now occupies. Then Venus will take over and sustain life. The vision showed me that life definitely could and does exist in other worlds and areas of the galaxy and the entire Universe.

The only world that I actually remember was a type of water world. The entire world was water and all of the living creatures were water based. There was no land and no cities. There were no buildings or material objects. It was like a warm bath in which we all existed and there was no worry, anger, or hate. There was only the warm love of the unity of the Creator, and the Creator's thoughts of us as the Creator's children.

Weston: Beyond the place that you know as Earth and the realities that you have here are infinite corridors to other realities. There are intergalactic gateways that you can enter if you know how. There are cities that are pure energy and there are other beings, too. Some of them look a lot like humans. Others look very different. I have a lot of friends in other worlds. They teach me about everything.

When you leave your body you are free from all of the dense matter that holds you to the Earth. Your consciousness is not limited, so you can go where you want. Your travels are not limited to places. You can visit other times too. Also, you can transform your energy to keep your balance in any of these places or times. Transforming your energy is as easy as breathing. Doing this is a lot like what some people call "shapeshifting." You just imagine that you are something and you become it.

Once you have learned how to shift your energy field, you become unlimited in where or when you can go. Traveling as a being of light releases you from physical limitations. You can become the birth of a star or the end of a world. You can ride the rhythms of the energy planes or stop in for visits in other worlds. For the most part, people in the other worlds are not only really nice, they care a lot about us on Earth. They are very troubled that we are such destructive creatures on Earth. They are really worried about the damage we are doing to our planet. In addition to that, they are frustrated with us because we don't realize that because of the law of cause and effect, everything that happens on Earth travels energetically and affects everyone and everything else on all other planes of reality. Everything is energy so everything is related harmonically.

There are very wise beings in some of those places. There are councils that monitor all life, all creation. They are very serious and stern, but at the same time they are only love. It is hard to describe, but very real. Some of the council members have books with lists of everyone who has ever lived. These are the books of names. In those books are the God names of everyone who has ever existed, all of the lives they have chosen, and the accomplishments and challenges that they have had.

There is also something that I call the *Book of Dreams*. In that book are all of the possibilities of every outcome of everything that everyone ever does. When we act there is always a reaction. With every reaction there is a chain of events that can go in any direction depending upon what is chosen next, so the possibilities are infinite. When we live human lives we don't really understand that we aren't bound by human rules or principals. There are much higher laws that we really live by. Those laws are of the One.

The One is the collective whole of all creation. Within that is a forever of choices. In those choices is the potential for the highest possible outcome. Human beings don't realize that their choices are unlimited.

Traveling outside of our bodies is a lot of fun, but at the same time has responsibilities. It isn't just an awesome ride. It is unlimited opportunity. If you realize that you can go from one time to another, because you are really living all times at the same time, you can make choices that literally change the reality that you live now, and at the same time that reality changes all of your other realities forever.

There is a lot of work to do beyond the Earthly life. There is a requirement of balance. Because of all of the constant changes that go on, energy builds on some levels of reality, while it might become depleted in others. There is light energy, which is ultimately the energy of God. We are all part of that energy. There is also dark energy that is very heavy. Those two energies constantly battle to be the greatest in all ways. Neither really can be, so there is a natural balance that occurs.

Also, on a physical plane, there is balance required for actual survival. When you travel from one parallel universe to the next, what you will find is that there are equalizers that add energy to one universe while draining the excess out of others. One form of these are black holes. If there weren't black holes the universe that you know would explode into nothingness. Because there are many different types of balancing mechanisms, energy is always moving. All of reality is really one big living organism that has a pulse and a life that is infinite.

Tristan: All of my life, I have visited other dimensions, other galaxies. The beings are very peaceful and loving, just like God.

Rhianna: In my out-of-body travels, I remember visiting a place with a kaleidoscope where you could see anything. I saw when Mom was a child and I read her diary! Out-of-body travel makes me smarter. I go to special places and learn from Spirit Teachers; they teach me about science, about how to be fit, and how to have fun!

Nathan: My spirit traveled to heaven when I was asleep. When I'm in heaven I go to a lot of planets.

Q: Jasin, are there other realities besides our Earth reality?

Jasin: Yes! Lots and lots, thousands and thousands, millions and millions. They are millions of galaxies away. I don't know why, but I don't know what they are like. I can tell you what Luvezorite feels like. If you want to know, all you have to do is say "Love." It is the color of turquoise. The turquoise we find here was brought from my planet. A humungous turquoise rock was tossed into a deep, deep hole. We need to have the turquoise inside of us to feel love.

Joseph: I think that we should give them no fear of what they have. That's all I think.

Scott: I kinda answered that already. Everything is mechanical except for the plants and rocks and those basic things.

Ahn: There are many worlds beyond this world. I have visited both sides; I've gone to lower worlds and to a place where there is just intense love floating in the air. What I have learned is that thoughts are things, but visions speak louder. Everything is always meant to be, for the highest good. Our Guardian Angels are always with us.

Q: Scotty, you get different realities in your dreams, don't you? Earlier when we were talking, you told me about a particularly important dream that you had in which you met someone and learned some very important things, right?

Scotty: I'm very connected to the ocean and we don't have one here in New Mexico, so I always have the ocean in my dreams. This time, I was walking toward these big rocky crags, and as I walked closer to them a mermaid came out. She had jet-black hair and instead of the regular mermaid body, it was like an eel. I interpreted her as a "dark" mermaid.

I walked up to her and she said, "Tell me a story."

So I started to tell her a story, and I started by saying, "Once upon a time there was a boy named Scott and he had a wonderful life but he wanted to be whole and to be connected." And I said a few more things and then I just snapped up out of my bed and I was like, "Well...I wasn't done telling my story, why is my dream done now?" And then all of a sudden it hit me. We have to be both dark and light, both all and nothing, both masculine and feminine, and then when we have all those things we'll be One.

And so I wrote this poem that says that you have to be everything, up and down, masculine and feminine, light and dark, and then at the very end it says "I am One."

The thing that was so amazing about the whole experience was that she made me discover that on my own. She didn't tell me anything; all she asked me to do was tell her a story, and so I talked about the first thing that popped in my head.

The really amazing thing is that all of the information within the Universe is within us. We could sit in a meadow for our entire lives and know everything that is going on if we would just be willing to discover what is in us.

Gabriel: I have a strong feeling there are others out there reaching out to us, but I cannot tell who they are.

Lindsay: There has to be...we are only 6 billion small...I refuse to believe that we are completely alone in a gigantic space. There are more dimensions and planes out there; we have yet to even scratch the surface. From what I have experienced I think they are pretty amazing.

6

Well the truth is
that I am out of my body
more than I am in it.
Living in other worlds
is easy for me.

—Weston

111

TRAVELING OUTSIDE
of OUR BODIES

Generally, having the awareness that there are other worlds and other beings outside of third-dimensional reality also means that the children are adept at traveling outside of their bodies. In other words, projecting their consciousness; leaving their bodies and traveling into other dimensional realities, past or future times; intergalactic traveling, including wormholes and parallel universes, as well as unlimited other venues.

For those who are adept, this sort of travel is as easy as breathing for the rest of us. It is often spontaneous and purely natural for an unfettered consciousness. Some adults are able to travel intentionally outside of their bodies as well, but most had to work at the skill either through meditation or other methods. For others, the ability came about through a spontaneous awakening. For the kids, it is a natural state of being.

Weston, who has participated in this work, has been visiting me and others for years. To experience the power of his consciousness as he enters your mind and literally changes your reality to what he wants you to see is mind-blowing the first couple of times. Imagine going about your business when all of a sudden BOOM! Your reality is no longer yours! What was just in your brain has disappeared, and now you are experiencing an entirely new reality—someone elses!

Awhile back I was in the recording booth at my friend Barry Goldstein's recording studio, Think Big Productions in New York City, where we were recording a CD for kids called "Inside and Out." Basically, the CD is a guided inner journey for kids to help them find their fears, problems, and worries, and to let go of them. Then, they continue the guided journey to find their inner gifts. As we recorded the session, I took the children on an inner exploration that entailed opening colorful boxes. In each box was a positive attribute.

One of those qualities is, of course, their imagination. I was in the process of telling the children that the imagination box was empty, and could never be full because their imagination is endless, when all of a sudden, the pictures in my head changed from what I was thinking to a colorful box that was full of frogs! The frogs were jumping out of the box, all over the place! And they made noise too! "Ribbit! Ribbit!"

Of course as soon as I got over the surprise of the reality shift, I realized who was behind it!

"Weston, geeze, I am working here!" And boy did he laugh! And the frogs kept coming. "Ribbit! Ribbit!" As they did, he laughed even more. I started to giggle and did so during the rest of the recording session. It was so cute that I left the giggles in the final CD version of the story.

Distance has no boundaries or effect on this type of phenomenon. Weston was in fact more than 3,000 miles away at the time! He is a powerful example of many of the new Evolution Children.

The degree of consciousness freedom that the kids have varies from child to child. Personally, I feel that this is a fabulous gift that should be encouraged. Who knows where our children can take us. On the other hand, some of these kids are so good at out-of-body travel and telepathy that I have had to set boundaries with them. What I mean is, to tell them not to interrupt me when I am in the middle of working or talking with someone else. Just because the children can do cool things doesn't mean that they shouldn't be taught good manners!

When the children communicate with others in other realities, they are often out of body. They can visit the past and the future, and even see themselves as they were in previous lives. They travel to other planets, or even back to the light, and as one of the boys said, to become regenerated.

One of the things that happens in relation to the giftedness of the Children of Now is that people tell them their stories aren't real, or that they aren't possibly capable of what they are saying. I assure you that it is all true. Well, okay, most of it. Kids do have huge imaginations! Here is how I put the question to them:

Q: **What have you learned in your out-of-body travels, or what have you remembered? Can we learn things from events that have happened or are happening in other dimensions? What? How does out-of-body travel help you?**

Jude: I have died and come back. This is what people call O.B.E—out-of-body experience. I was at an after-hours party at a friend's house in Boston, and we were doing things that we shouldn't have regarding certain substances. I overdid it. My body felt light, light, lighter, and then I was floating above it looking down on the scene. I was lying on the couch and looking up with blue-tinted lips and a white face.

I remembered looking at the corner of the room as I lifted out of my body. The corner started to swirl like a whirlpooling effect. Behind the wall there was nothing but white. The center of the whirlpool was a black dot, and it was sucking reality into it. Then I floated very high into the ethereal plane. I could still see the living room and couch that was far below me. I then also could see everyone that was on the planet. I felt as though I could be everywhere or anywhere that I wanted with a thought. I was everywhere but nowhere. It was a very loving yet paradoxical feeling.

As I drifted higher and higher all around me, I could see white. Then I reached a level where I was no longer drifting up. I then started to move forward on what seemed to be a "people mover," much like the ones they have in an airport; however, I could not see my body, and I believe that at the time I had no body. They call that the "floating-head feeling."

As I moved forward on this conveyor belt that I could not see I began to hear speaking in tongues. I was shown or told by some claircognizance what the tongues actually were. They are every spoken language, every thought process, and every emotion of every living and nonliving being in the area of the mass consciousness stream of the Earth and our solar system.

I was also shown that other solar systems with sentient beings have their own mass consciousness that is on different levels than ours. The sound is hard to explain in writing; however, I am able to recreate it with my voice as if it happened yesterday. It was all languages but no language, and again it is one of the ultimate paradoxes of life.

I then saw a huge swirling mass of energies that was translucent in nature. It was shimmering with all colors, like a mother of pearl. I was told that this was, in visual form, the mass consciousness of Earth. It was around me like a ring of fire. A very thick ring. I began to travel through it and as I did my emotions changed.

It felt like I was taken out of a warm bath for my human experience, and this was the point where I was returning to the warm waters of love that the Creator provides after death. I was traveling through it. The entire time whiteness was all around me. That is why it is hard for me when people say they are in a tunnel with a white light at the end. I was in a tunnel of pure white light and shimmering energies with a black dot at the far end that increased in size as I traveled on the people mover of the soul's next journey. As I got closer and closer to the black dot at the end of the mover I could see that there were galaxies upon galaxies within the space of the black dot at the end.

I was told that I was approaching the waiting area to the crystal city where I would review my past, present, and future lives; however, when I could make out the stars in the blackness ahead, the people mover started to reverse. I was told it was not my time; that I had a message to spread around the Earth, and I was given another gift that would help me to achieve this soul goal.

I was given an astral cord to that portal. It was much like the astral cord that you use when you travel on the astral plane; but instead, it was for the people that go and come from the land of the living to that of the dead and back to living again. The astral cord is used by the other side to instant message me when they need me to know something or help with something. It is also used when I go into sleep mode or unconscious states to let my future self in this life come in and bring my soul to do light work.

I am not sure what I do when I do this work; however, I do know that it is my purpose and future self that is pulling me to do it. I go out of body a lot since that instance; however, it is always when I am asleep and I do not remember a lot of it. The only thing that I have been told and remember is that there is a council around me watching me. They are of a different dimension, and I sense that it is where my soul energy was birthed from the Creator. I have been told that it may be Nuevo; however, I am unsure at this point. I wake up tired and aching even though I have had 12 hours or more of sleep; that is how I know that it has happened.

I know that I am helping people that I have met in the present, past, and future. I am unsure of what I am doing; however, their lives always seem to improve. I act as a catalyst, and in the future I am sure I will uncover what I was doing in the present with my present self. I do remember a room. It contained a large, round table that seemed like it was small, yet could fit every member of the council.

This council represents a being of every species within the entire Universe. We sit at this large table in a very brightly lit room. The colors are white and off-white. We close our eyes and sit in the circle and seem to be meditating, and then the council begins. They review information from the key souls that are present. They confer over the information. Then they lovingly tell us what we need to do in our lives to prevent an event that must not happen.

I am unsure what the council is, who they represent, and what we are discussing, but the synchronicities within my life and my gifts only get stronger every time I feel that I was sitting in council. The chakra that I received as a messaging device was once part of us in our Atlantean and Lemurian lives that I have been told and confirmed. I know that there are others that can describe in better detail about this council, and I hope to find them someday.

Weston: Well the truth is that I am out of my body more than I am in it. Living in other worlds is easy for me. Part of me lives away from my physical body all of the time. That is what I am most used to. There are unlimited places to go and people and other beings to meet beyond the world that you know. A lot of them have many things to teach from their experience, because humans aren't really that old in comparison to other beings in other dimensions and the worlds there.

I like to travel with my friends. They make me laugh and we have a lot of fun. Besides that, there are places that I go where I can make a huge difference in the balance of the worlds. I also learn about harmonic vibrations and energy. I use those harmonics to call out to the infinite for the changes that are coming. Not just to call for those changes, but to ease them in vibrationally so that there isn't chaos when the changes come. That is a really big job, but I know that I am making a difference.

Often when I am out of my body I visit people. Lots of those people can see or hear me. I just transmute my energy to match their energy fields and hop right in. I laugh when it startles people. I laugh even more when they can see me, because that makes me happy. I visit Dr. Meg, and others too. My Aunt

Carmen and I have a lot of fun together outside of our bodies. Dr. Meg and I have had some great adventures too, like the time we went to Atlantis together. I showed her parts of Atlantis that she has never seen. It was fun. What was really fun was when I took Dr. Meg to meet my soul mate. Her name is Nahlah. We got to her house right after she was born and she remembered me. I am so happy to see her. We travel together out of our bodies all of the time. Even though she is in another time and another place that doesn't matter because we can be together outside of dense reality. She is a very advanced soul, and I often have to work to keep up. She often gives me those looks when I remember some things. But she is patient with me.

There are beings who visit me too, especially at night. They really frighten me because they are ugly. When they come I panic and run to my mom. They look like dog people with wrinkly faces and skin. They have great big mouths and little tiny ears. They just stand there and stare at me and I don't like that. They come in the bathroom, too. Sometimes they look in the windows. Other people can't see them, but they are real. I don't know why they come. Dr. Meg calls them the Watchers. She and my Aunt Carmen can usually make them go away, but they always come back.

I have special people who watch me now and keep me safe. They are very ancient. They are very formal when they are around. They have protocol that is very important to them. They have a reverence for tradition and ceremony. Somehow this makes them very powerful. When they are around I do feel like a little boy. Aunt Carmen calls these guys the Mayans because of how they look. Like Mayan warriors.

When I am out of my body and traveling in other dimensions and parallel universes, the colors and the textures of reality are very different depending on where I am. I have watched stars being born and other stars die. I have visited lots of different planets with very different environments. There is one planet that is all purple and pink, even the air. There is another one that is all silvery blue, and others too that are very beautiful and don't look like Earth at all. There are other realities that aren't a form, or dense, but all like air, yet there they are, whoever inhabits those dimensions. Usually those people are the ones who teach me. They make the energy big and then it fills me up and I just know things. Instant learning. Not like schoolwork!

Sometimes I go to the light to get recharged. That is important because since I am all electromagnetic when I am outside of my body, the static that happens as I move through the various realities wears down my field sometimes so I need to regenerate. I like going to the Light because it is what is inside of me. It is my real home.

Tristan: When I was really little, I had a lot of people come to me who had just died. They were on their way to the Spirit World. Sometimes they were children, so we would play with my toys until the Angels came for them. The Angels were always so beautiful and loving. I also had a dying dog visit with me one time. I think what I learned from this was that dying isn't scary, because there are always loving Angels and Spirits helping you through that time.

A few years ago, I began flying with a very tall alien woman. There were other aliens on the spaceship, but I mostly talked (in my mind) to her. The spaceship was a cylinder shape, which flew vertically. It was very bright. The alien woman was very nice. The first time I flew with her, the woman said she was sad because so many people were being killed on Earth. She then had me watch a really large TV screen that showed the war in Iraq. I didn't like seeing all the killing, so I told the woman that I had seen enough and to please turn it off. She turned it off and then we all made a circle around a bright, white light, held hands, and sent healing energy to Earth.

Q: Tristan, do you have any idea who these beings are?

Tristan: Two of the beings are my parents who live on another planet. When they visit me on Earth, they take on a body form filled with bright, white light. When I fly and visit them, then we all look like balls of white light. They give me energy so I can feel calmer on Earth, because I feel a lot of people's negative feelings.

We talk in our minds together and also use a language of symbols, sort of like some of the crop circle designs. It's kind of hard for me to remember these symbols. They just started coming into my mind lately, and I know that is how we communicated, but I can't remember exactly what they look like. Maybe I will remember them later. We talk about how to keep good energy in me. I cannot always remember what they tell me to do, but usually what happens is my mom finds someone to teach us energy work like Reiki and Qigong and other things that can help me feel better. Qigong really helps me feel better the most.

The alien woman I have been flying with for a few years is very tall and wears a long robe. The robe has a symbol on it that looks kind of like a Y, but the Y doesn't go down in the middle. It has a straight line that connects the two slanted lines. There is a circle around that shape. Her face is really kind and she has a nice smile. She has beautiful, bright blue eyes. All the contact I have is with her; there are other aliens around, but mostly in the background. I don't see them too much. She flies in a cylinder-shape spaceship. From the outside it looks like it is all lit up with bright white light. I think it flies just with some type of energy and not fuel. It doesn't make any noise at all when it flies.

The very first time I flew with her I remember that she was very sad. She showed me the Iraq War on the TV screen. She held my left hand in her right hand and a door opened up in the bottom of the spaceship in front of our feet. We were sitting down. I could see the Earth through this door and we began to send healing energy to Earth through our hands. We have done this a few times, but she hasn't shown me the movie screen of people being killed anymore because she knows how upset I became. That was very sad.

Other times we have picked up other children from Earth who she said could also learn to send healing energy to Earth. They were really scared, and I helped them feel more comfortable. I hadn't flown with her in a while because it was getting so difficult to function here on Earth. So I talked (in my mind) to the alien woman and told her the problems I was having; she said that I didn't have to fly with her anymore, and, when I get older, maybe I could come with her again. She also told me that I could still send the healing energy to Earth by using visualizations in my meditations. I also taught my mom and dad to do this, too. My mom, dad, and I went to a Qigong workshop and they taught us how to send Qigong healing energy to Earth. This is good for everyone to do. I know I go to other dimensions but I don't remember them too much—I mean, what they look like. I just remember flying through dark tunnels to get to these places. I know that the planets in these other galaxies are different colors. They are really beautiful. I just remember flying around with other beings of light and it feels really great. The other beings are so loving and there is never any war. I think that is because they do not see each other as being different, but know that they are all a part of the light.

I also fly a lot with the whales in the Universe. I really like that a lot. They are so beautiful. My dad and I call them "gentle giants." So far I don't remember if they are communicating to me, but I just know it is so wonderful and peaceful to be with them. Sometimes here on Earth I feel so anxious because of all the energy that isn't so good, so I think the whales really help me feel more relaxed.

I had a dream about healing with dolphins. I was walking on a boat dock and saw about seven dolphins lying on a fishing boat. I held up my hands and sent healing energy to them. One of them was able to get back into the water, but it had an anchor stuck in his tail. I jumped in the water and saw the dolphin flip its fin around until the anchor was out. The dolphin then began to sing the most beautiful song, in its mind, to the other dolphins. I think it was a healing song, because the other dolphins on the boat began to wake up, and all of them were able to make it back into the water. It was so wonderful to see them jumping and swimming in the water. They are so loving.

I don't know how they could just be left on the boat to die.

Christina: When I travel out of body, I like to travel to the place where my Guides are. In this dimension I still have the appearance of a human, but traveling to different parts takes a split second, which I like because I don't like waiting. My Guides take the form of dragons, because they are a source of power and protection for me. Communication between us feels like vibrations, almost like when you hear a different language, but you understand it without having to translate in your head.

Q: Can we learn things from events that have happened or are happening in other dimensions? What? How does out-of-body travel help you?

Christina: Out-of-body travel help me most when I feel stressed in my physical body, or when I don't know which direction to take. I can communicate with them and know that there is no judgment. I would help other people with out-of-body travel to show them that there is the physical world, but there are also other worlds that are beautiful places and there is so much to explore.

Jasin: I can not answer that. Out-of-body travel is not traveling. It is waking up. There is no such thing as going to sleep, because you are waking up on Earth—the real Earth. The one that is nice and peaceful.

Joseph: I can see above myself, and yes, one time I was not too far from my body, but I was definitely above it and I could see myself. I could see everyone, everywhere. I could, as I was looking down, I could see the colors of their Aura at the time.... Their main colors. I could see myself in the crowd and I could see people singing at the stage in the cafeteria. It was green, the audience was blue, and I was purple, but I think that I created that in my mind because I can create it; so I understand it, so I think that was what it was. I think that I was out of my body and seeing down, seeing everything from a different view.

Scott: The thing that I have learned is that fighting over something or declaring war is not the answer and logic cannot prove everything. Logic is just a shadow, and from what I remember, we should try our best to stay positive...or else. If we don't, it usually leads to bad things happening.

Q: Can we learn things from events that have happened or are happening in other dimensions? What? How does out-of-body travel help you?

Scott: Yes you can. You can learn alternative ways to tell what you want instead of declaring war or whining about it. When bad things happen to you, out-of-body travel helps you to forget those bad things and keep you on the positive, unless you don't allow it.

Ahn: Out-of-body traveling is just phenomenally amazing! It helps me not to just wallow in my physical pity, it helps me to look outside the box and know that I always have Divine company on higher levels with me. I have certain guides who fly with me in my dream state and I also go places, see things, and bring back messages. In February 2007, while out of body and in dream state, I saw a man holding a newspaper and the front page had a picture of a big ship broken and sinking and the numbers (or date) on top which read 777. I wasn't sure what this meant, but I told my mother about this dream and a few days later she found out that Al Gore was launching an S.O.S. (Ship Sinking) "Live Earth" concert on July 7, 2007 (777) on 7 continents to raise awareness of how we've been treating Mother Earth and what we can do to change this.

In a recent dream I was with many people and we were gathered in a circle. Encircling us were lots and lots of trees that all had eyes. The eyes of the trees and the eyes of the people were light colors, like orange, purple, red, yellow—some having one color and some being multicolored. Instead of a black pupil, the center of the eye was white. After we gazed into someone's eyes and then looked away, we would experience pure pleasure or healing where needed in the body. I love eyes, so this was a powerful dream to me.

Gabriel: I have an image of seeing a body in a rocking chair. It helps me to remember we do not live forever.

Lindsay: Well I believe that I travel every night after I fall asleep. I am not too sure that I remember too much from my out-of-body experiences that have directly affected my life in ways that I can measure. My main dimensional lessons come from conversing with others in those dimensions. Out-of-body travel has never really been my chosen path. I work more as a translator for beings from the other sides.

7

We are not ordinary people.
We are extraordinary people.
And that is why we can feel and give love so freely.
It's one of those gifts that everyone has.
The ability to love is, and always *will* be.

—Lindsay

DOVE
©Lyrics by Ahn van Mentz
February 11, 2007

Get in touch with your dove
To know more about unconditional love
See through and through
To the magnificent you
The powerful soul
That has been always whole

Stretching my arms out wide
Getting an ache on my left side
My thoughtful side hasn't been touched
Sensing a crying on how much it's crushed
My aches and pains
Are feeling the game

Get in touch with your dove
To know more about unconditional love
See through and through
To the magnificent you
The powerful soul
That has been always whole

Running around
Afraid to fall down
Too frightened to give it up
My Olympic cup
Let go, and be free
Why strive? . . . Just BE!

Get in touch with your dove
To know more about unconditional love
See through and through
To the magnificent you
The powerful soul
That has been always whole

WHAT IS LOVE?

ove. What is it really? Is it just an emotion or something more? As human beings we spend all or most of our lives just looking for love, fantasizing about it, feeling that we need and want it, that it will be our answer to who we are. For some of us, we look to love to find our value, our fullness, and a myriad of other untruths. Love has become idealized to the point where many people no longer know what it feels like to truly be loved, or what loving another person is really about.

Love, in many ways, seems to have lost its depth. It has become about things and stuff, even commercialized. Love is far beyond the romanticized, idealized perceptions we have developed.

To this author, love is a way of being—spontaneity unconditionally born of the innocence of an open heart. Love is every particle of which we are created, and each of these wondrous particles are borne of the light from which we were made. Inherently, we are love. Love is us.

As I move about the world, traveling from one place to the next, it is my observation that we don't seem to honor people outside of ourselves. Even the people we say we love the most. We don't honor people in general, and we often don't know how to love ourselves.

I wanted the children to talk about love, because they have that innocence we have lost. The responses from the children on this topic were nearly unanimous. Not surprising really, but the wisdom that came with their common thread directly targets the heart and soul and succeeds with a direct hit! It was here, with this question, that the children really got onto familiar and comfortable ground with me, and their true selves began to shine through!

Here is how I put the question to the children:

Q: **What is love as it applies to our lives? In other words, what is REAL love and how can we as ordinary people bring that into our world?**

Nicholas: I love this question about love. I like to answer from the perspective most people can relate. Love is what we feel when we feel our hearts gush. Now I did not say make mush. Simply, the feeling when our hearts feel joy, tenderness, and harmony at the same time. It is the feeling we have when we feel in our hearts a complete opening of love when a baby is born.

Real love is like the tickle on your toes—you know it when you feel it. It is like an undeniable sensation of splendor. It leaves you feeling tickled pink.

Q: How do we get there Nicholas?

Nicholas: We can bring this REAL love feeling into our lives through first being aware of our heart energy. It comes in many forms and reminds us throughout the day to tell us it is there.

When our heart speaks, all we need to do is listen. Talk to it, ask it how it is. Be prepared for an answer. This answer is a mighty lesson for us to follow. Regular dialogue, such as telling your heart how much you love it and listening, opens up this channel. Of course there are other ways beyond the context of this question.

Q: One of the ways that children like you find healing and balance is through nature. How can we apply this love of nature to "real life"? How can we respect the integrity of nature while living in an industrialized world?

Nicholas: God wants us to be in alignment with each of our purposes. If we stray from this purpose, we create such subliminal deviation from planetary mission.

We are at this place in history due to invention, which is God given. Yes we need to be in harmony with this. If humans truly listen to nature, they would not suggest anything that goes against love for all life. Again, people like scientists can experiment, yet it needs to be in harmony with God's original intent.

Grandma Chandra: Love is an emotion experienced by humans. REAL love comes from Source or Creator.

Q: How can we experience the difference?

Grandma Chandra: We can experience this by opening our crown chakras to receive this love and send it out through our heart chakras to all beings.

Q: Jude how do you remind yourself to experience real love as opposed to the idealized type?

Jude: When I need to be reminded what the REAL feeling of love is, I do a visualization exercise. It is not that I do not know the feeling, but to get it into my being in the easiest way possible I use my ability of visualization. I close my eyes and I think back to when I was alone and depressed as a junior in college.

I was alone in my dorm room and didn't have a significant other to spend my time with. Love with another person seemed unobtainable at that time in my life. So even though I was not supposed to, I went out and got a kitten! I think back to that very first day when I went out searching for the right kitten; it had to be a free one. And there he was, the last one left in the litter. I knew that he was supposed to be my companion and the love that I was missing at that time.

To get that real love feeling all I have to do is to think back on that day and visualize what it felt like when I first held him in my arms and looked down at the tiny, furry gray face that I called Spaz. It was that "awww" feeling that touched my heart that day, and that was also the feeling of true unconditional love. That is real love. Nonjudgmental and totally unconditional.

Q: So once we have love, how do we bring it to the world?

Jude: It is not until you can have those two in perfect combination that you, at least how I see it, will know the feeling of true love. To bring it into the world faster and in more frequency we need to stop judging others, to stop placing conditions on the love we receive and give to others, and to be completely open to all the different types and forms love can come in.

Love is not perfect; however, if you live in and about love, you are closer to that perfect spark that is the Creator and the place that we originated from— that pure, true, real, and Divine love.

Q: Do you feel like there is a way that everyone can get to the place of unconditional love?

Jude: There is no way at this present point that the majority of the world will be able to awaken to this love, unless there is a earth-shattering event that causes us all to forget color, religion, and differences. We need to celebrate the likeness that we all share in the human race and then, and only then, will we become one with the Universe and the Earth.

When your heart vibrates and pulsates its language through your body as the heat from the breath of life itself, then you will know the true feeling of the real and only universal love.

Weston: Love is the epitome of embracing perfection. It is when you are being yourself, because then you have *acknowledged* your perfection; and honestly, perfection can't be anything less than itself because it comes from God, the Creator.

Love is not just a romantic notion. That kind of love is purely emotional. Love is really a way to be. A *state* of being. When you deny your true selves, you deny the truth of who you really are. Who you are is much greater than what you think. You are forever; borne of creation, contributive to the One that provides constancy of all life.

Q: So how do we get there?

Weston: When you have *become* love, you have accepted your place amongst the One. And that is contagious. When you live as love, what happens is that other people begin to respond to you. They see and feel your light. And they can't help but to light up too. The problem is some people think that showing their light leaves them vulnerable, so they don't do it. The truth is that showing your light means that you *have* shed your vulnerabilities, and that is when you are in truth.

In order to truly love you have to *be* love.

Tristan: Love comes from our hearts. Sometimes I feel upset and angry, and that energy gets stuck in my body, so I am not in a good mood.

Q: So when that happens, how do you get back to love?

Tristan: When I mediate or do Qigong it helps me remember the loving energy I have inside. Maybe these things could help other people be more loving too.

Peter: Real love is that you don't hate anything and everything is good. Just be positive and avoid negative thoughts.

Q: How about you, Christina?

Christina: Real love is a feeling of joy and connection with everything and everyone. Real love would be unconditional love, when there is no judgment and every aspect of life is accepted and appreciated and beautiful. To bring it into your life, just be grateful for what you have and what you are going to have. Try to turn everything into a positive; for example, if you can't get work done around the house, realize that you have a home, and many people around the world don't.

Jasin: We *are* love. Everything is love. It applies as everything. We don't have to bring it because it is already in us. We are bringing it no matter what. The cord that connects us when we are sleeping is like a satellite. We collect love when we are sleeping and when we wake up—we send it out. We are doing it no matter what.

Joseph: Love affects us by bringing joy and happiness when we send unconditional love to even those we dislike. It spreads more love to our world, helping it become more peaceful with more truth and honesty and love. So that's pretty much it.

Q: Scott?

Scott: I'm stumped on that one.

Ahn: To bring love into this world is first loving ourselves, and when our love cup is overflowing we are able to give love, and because nobody can hold love, love is forever flowing; it will flow all around Mother Earth and Father Sky.

Q: Gabriel, what is real love?

Gabriel: Love is when you see the inside of things where they matter. We all need to learn the inner beauty that is in us and how other people's beauty speaks to us. What people are trying to say is reflected back to us when we love.

Lindsay: I think you like asking all of these unanswerable questions.... *Real* love? Again it's a feeling you can't put into words. It's a picnic on a summer day; it's those amazing cookies your grandmother bakes; its those big, pick-you-up hugs that only your dad can give and those sweet, tender hugs from your mom; its your very first kiss and your very last dance. Love is everywhere and everything. Love isn't just a romantic, mushy moment between two people. It's drinking coffee at five in the morning with your partner, or eating s'mores over an open fire.

We are not ordinary people. We are extraordinary people. And that is why we can feel and give love so freely. It's one of those gifts that everyone has. The ability to love is, and always *will* be.

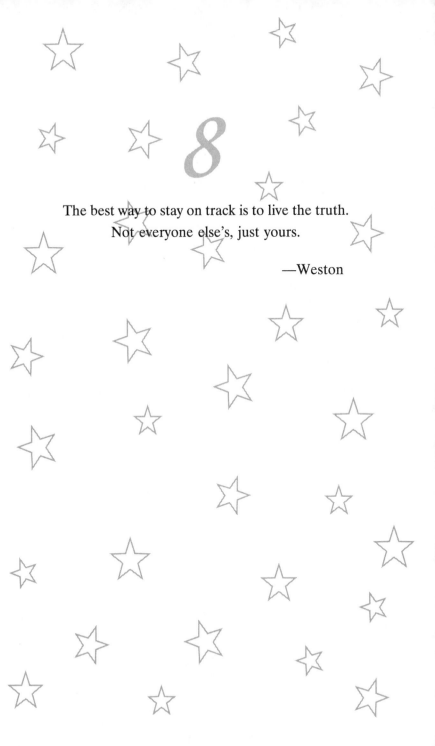

8

The best way to stay on track is to live the truth.
Not everyone else's, just yours.

—Weston

BECOMING FULFILLED

In today's world we have become desensitized. There is so much information coming at us so fast that we barely have time to consciously process it before the next wave comes.

The entire world has become competitive, and, with the Internet and mass media, we have a minute-by-minute, blow-by-blow description of what is happening everywhere in our world on a real-time basis. Sometimes the amount of information creates so much drama that we become completely overwhelmed.

We are being pushed to do more, to be more. The ads we see, no matter what form of media, tell us that if we have this or look like that then we are a success. We have become a world of haves and have-not's. There is a wide gap between the two, and neither end of the spectrum appears to be truly happy. Everyone is seeking that which they don't have, and what they don't have is mostly a sense of self. They have lost their passion and don't know who they are inside because there is such a montage of information in there.

With all of that comes a feeling of emptiness. As if there is something missing from life.

My perception is that most people are searching for what fills them, for who they are in this vast and fast moving world. Most everyone just wants the truth and how it relates to them, but with all of the input we have, that can be hard to recognize.

In my humble observation, the solution to this issue is to stop looking outside of ourselves and look inside to get to know ourselves, our inner truth, our fears, and our desires. It is to embrace the perfection inside of us, of which we are created, and finally, to accept who we are, what we are, and whatever that might look like along the vast miles of our inner journeys. I often tell people the two words that will change their lives are: "I accept."

These words cannot be said from the mind, but must come from the heart. What I realized somewhere along the way was that we do a lot of our inner healing in our heads, from a mental perspective, but that healing never takes place on deeper levels because it didn't come from the heart. In fact, the only way to become healed and fulfilled is from the perspective of our hearts.

I thought I would ask the kids what their perceptions were about this subject.

Q: **These days, people feel empty inside as if something is missing. How can they get back in touch with that part of themselves that really hasn't gone anywhere?**

Nicholas: I understand that many people feel empty due to their disillusion from their true self. The true self is the self that they have come here to know, yet have been pulled away from their core, through distraction. When we look at the core of any human being, we will see the essence of love as only a baby knows it.

I have come to know my core as the holy center and will of God. I see this place as the place where God's love imbues and anoints me. It is a sacred place from which my body form has manifested. If we can remain clear that Divine Source Energy is a constant source of unyielding supply there for us to know, we can become more affirmed that this love is always there for us.

My suggestion for the many people who desire to leave their empty or depressive state is to quietly revisit the Source Energy we all came from. I believe feelings of emptiness can leave as soon as we can live in the moment with the glorified energy of God.

Jude: This would be to find themselves and the Divine spark that is within all life. Inner power needs to be taken, grown, and used to bring the reality and thoughts of God and your higher self to the physical realm of Earth and the Universe. There is an inner journey that needs to be sought out by all those that are feeling empty.

They tend to navigate toward religions; however, that is not the correct movement in my views and senses. That is a good beginning; however, people need to search across many religions until they have a balanced sense of the truth amongst all the religions of the Earth. It is only through a healthy combination of the truths of all religions that encompass the planet Earth that they will begin the inner seeking of Divine truths and the connections that they can only gain with their higher self and soul through self-explorative activities.

People need to find their life purposes and their hidden passions in this life. They need to learn to unconditionally love, and to look at all beings and life through the same eyes of nonjudgment. There is no religion that can show God or yourself to you. The only person that can give you the truth is yourself. We all hold the seeds of the universe within our thoughts and souls; the seeds are currently going unwatered and wasted.

This is the emptiness that I sense these people are feeling. It is that they are not on the right track, they are not fulfilling their life purpose, and they have not discovered themselves or their true reason for being here in the NOW. The part of themselves that they need to discover is their higher selves, their soul selves, and their unity with the Divine as a seed of the Creator. Until they find these things, and place a majority of their thought process and energies into this self-explorative discovery, they will continue to feel the empty feeling that leads to severe levels of depression and self-destructive activities.

Again, many will flock to religion, and in the worst cases, cults; however, I stress that I sense and feel that these are not the answer. The self and the personal individual connection with the Creator is the answer. To find purpose is the answer. To live your life with purpose, dignity, reverence, and intent are the answers to the self-discovery process known as human life. These people are not using their emotions to discover the uniqueness of humanity. They are keeping them dormant, and that is what is creating their depression. Exercise the muscle of reality manifestation and self-discovery, and the emptiness will diminish and purpose will takes its place.

Weston: People think they are empty because they have not remembered that they are already perfect and already have everything that they need. Values have changed, and what people think is important is all part of the illusion.

The illusion is that achievements are important. That individuals are important. That there is nothing greater than self-fulfillment, which leads to emptiness, because it isn't true. The truth is that everything everyone is looking for is already inside of them. The truth is that there is no emptiness. Emptiness is just a perception. When people look outside of themselves for what they want, they are only getting the opinions of other people.

Those people have made decisions based on their experiences, and they might not have made very good ones. But whatever they did was their truth at the time. Even if they succeeded at whatever they decided, it doesn't mean someone else will because maybe it isn't the direction their life was meant to go. Or maybe they are just doing it because someone else did. When people do that it gets them into trouble.

The best way to stay on track is to live the truth. Not everyone else's, just yours.

Peter: Self-exploration and meditation!

Christina: Find something you love doing or a place you love to be, physical or not. Loving life can change the way you see everything; love can fill you with joy, and joy is one of my favorite experiences. When I ride dressage, I love every minute of it. The feeling of being connected with the horse and the smooth movements, the wind on my skin, and knowing that it is beautiful and natural.

Rhianna: People who feel empty need to believe in themselves and have faith.

Jasin: Unlock the drawer, practice, and then POOF—they have it! They just need to *use* it.

Q: What is it?

Jasin: Love....

Joseph: I think that people who feel empty are just missing love in their life, and it's partially due to the fact that they haven't sent love out. The fact that they haven't sent unconditional love and they bring so much, like complaining, thinking only on the bad side, brings them to think that they haven't been loved as much as they could. But they don't really know that.

Scott: I'm not sure. If you believe it's there...it's there.

Ahn: When people feel empty inside, they are feeling the illusion, because they have always been whole from the start. The one thing that I do to get in touch is sing my mantra and meditate, and do what I truly, deeply love, from my heart and soul.

Gabriel: Turn off the TV, go outside, and have a conversation with the neighbors and the trees.

Lindsay: I have often wondered what the solution is for the emptiness. I think it just takes some searching. It's easy to find something that really hasn't gone anywhere; you just have to want to find it. And I think that some people are too scared to actually know who they are.

Tristan: We have so much love inside of us, and if we share that with everyone we meet then we will never feel empty. I see people sometimes walking and they look so unhappy on their faces. If I smile and then they smile back we all feel so good inside and full of love. A couple of days ago my mom, dad, and I were talking while we were standing in line to buy some water. There was a nice man in front of us and he turned around and looked at us with a big smile on his face. We all were smiling back and it felt so good. When I see homeless people on the street, I do a Reiki symbol and send them energy. I hope this helps them feel better.

9

God isn't religion.

God isn't a stern figure who punishes us for doing something bad.

We punish ourselves enough without having to have God do it...

—Weston

☆☆☆

Sometimes I hear dark voices.

This is because I live in the light and there are things that try to test me away from the light, but that darkness is not God.

—Gabriel

CALLING ALL ANGELS
BY JUDE DECOFF
(©JUDE DECOFF, 2007)

I call my Angels to my side

They come without hesitation or pride

They are here to help, heal, and wonder

They hear my cries like a shot of thunder

My cries echo out across the night

They come to release me of fear and fright

I feel the wings of their angelic heritage

They try to help without the thought of lineage

They know the Father, the Creator the Divine

They ask you to remember the lost the hurt
and sublime

Healing will come they whisper in my ear

You may have to wait a minute, a week, a
month, or year

In the time of this, the waiting game

Is the time you need to be able to regain

Your personal power the thoughts and flowers

The beauty of life is found in the struggles
of strife

You will be fine the Angel did say

You will release your hurt your struggles
and pains

Release them all to the Divine through me

I will bring them to God and a solution you
shall see.

148

God Is...

Who, or what, is God? Does anybody know? How do we identify something or someone whom we have never seen? How do we even know that God exists? And if so, how does God apply to our lives, our journeys as human beings, to the love we seek with all of our hearts?

The concept of God is a personal thing. It is the lifeblood of many—their beliefs and the idea of what God wants guides and fills them. For others, it is a nebulous question with the intangible difficult to grasp, but there must be *something*.... Some higher power that dictates our experiences and gives us life. Many strive to please a vengeful God, while others grasp the ideal of a loving God who will provide, while others die for their God in idealistic martyrdom.

Is there more to God than we have been lead to believe? During the course of our history, religious documents, actual accounts of Old Testament and New Testament history, have been modified to suit the rulers of the time, such as when

Constantine had the Bible translated to his own liking and purposes. At other times, the Gnostics were considered to be heretics, and they hid their libraries of ancient teachings in caves to protect them. Some of those documents were discovered in jars in Qumran in the 1940s. They contained pure translations of Gospels that were not included in our modern version of the Bible.

Other documents have also been found that clearly contradict our current accepted versions of the Holy Bible.

It is not my position to judge who is or isn't right, or what we should believe. But perhaps there is more to our history than we have been taught. For instance, in my own awakening, I had many, many visions of geometric forms that floated before me. I found that when I projected my consciousness into those forms, I was absorbed with different aspects of knowledge.

Those experiences were powerful, as I learned not only entire concepts, but every detail all at once. I laughingly called it "learning by osmosis." Much of the information was verifiable while other parts of it were so beyond measurable science that they seemed more like full-bodied remembering. In "The Gospel of Truth," one of the writings that was found in a Qumran cave in the 1940s, there was a paragraph that described the very thing I experienced *more than 2,000 years later*. It was in that moment that I had a great "aha!" and realized that we are much more than we know.

The subject of God is a very personal one. I would not presume to decide what is right or not for anyone, and I will leave to everyone to identify their beliefs for him- or herself.

For the purpose of this book, I asked the children about God. I had a feeling that they would have answers that were inarguable, for they speak purely and lack judgment or prejudice. Their answers are stunning.

Q: **Who is God? Is God a person or something more? What is our relation to God? Is that relationship the same as religion or something more?**

Nicholas: From my perspective, God or Creator Source Energy is the inner sanctum of my cherished Being. It is the essence and fabric of my life. God is an overlay that I feel as I look upon the landscape of my life. It is a presence I recognize through my communion with all things. What wows me most of all is the availability of God for us at all times. This all-powerful, omniscient presence only asks that we honor this powerful presence for us to receive the highest assistance. Honoring means to give credence to; to cherish and respect its glory. For me, God is within the core of our Being and without as part of Divine consciousness of everything, yet cannot be described as a person. The magnitude of God encompasses so much more.

Our relationship to God is constantly changing as we directly affect all of creation through our habits of destruction. You see, as we devalue the landscape of the Earth, we, in each moment, change the honoring and respect we owe the Creative Source Energy that brought Earth together. Our amendment to this is through our heart centers being open and amplified as we meet and treat each other with honored loved and respect. You see, this love and respect we show each other is felt by the Earth's energy field and reverberated back to us.

Q: Does science have anything to do with God?

Nicholas: The relationship between science and religion is a direct unity of cohesive particles in all levels. By this I mean at a most infinitesimal level, particles are recognizing each other and able to operate with their different levels of vibration through the One Consciousness. On the one hand, scientists may think that they are only working with hard facts, data, and experiments, yet the truth is the whole planet Earth is working with hard facts, data, and experiments simultaneously. Therefore, the whole global Earth is one scientific experiment in the eyes and mind of God. So you see, there is a relationship between science and religion paralleling each other, while also religion (God) is an observer to science (planet Earth).

Q: Nicholas, how can scientists know God's original intent?

Nicholas: It is coming. For example, even as scientists deviate, they are still on track. They shall come to realize the error of their ways. "God" continues to speak loudly, and this in time will be heard.

Q: Grandma, who is God?

Grandma Chandra: God is a Source of Light (Knowledge); an energy, not a person. We are a part of God, Energy, Light, we are one Soul. Some people call it religion. Some people say it is a reunification with Creator Source through Ascension.

Q: Jude?

Jude: God is us. We are God. God is every molecule and intangible thought. God is every word written or spoken across all species and sentient beings across the Universe. God is a diamond. We are the facets of that large diamond, and all of our lives past, present, and future are the light that sparkles from facet. We are as much God as the keyboard that I am typing on at this very moment. It is a Oneness and paradoxical concept, and in that paradox exists God.

Q: Do you feel that God is a person?

Jude: God is not a person as far as I sense it. I sense God as a force that is known as Divine Order. Through God's thought processes galaxies are born. God thought of the Earth and it existed.

Q: What about religion? How does that fit with the concept of God?

Jude: Religion is humanity's attempt to explain the unexplainable known as God. Religion was designed more to control through fear—for example, the fear of Hell, which consequently does not exist in my beliefs. Through this taxation and control, the people were stifled, and their real concepts and beliefs of God were cast away as Paganism and Witchcraft.

In the religious revolution and creation stages in our world—which, in my views, began with the founding of America—the Protestant religions, the Jesuits, and the Spanish explorers defied and combated the old religions of the more Earth-based peoples of the world, such as the Aztecs, Myans, Incans, Druids, Pagans, and other nonsecular religions that failed to hold the structure and power of the Catholic and Protestant branches at those specific times in the world's history.

It was when church, money, and government were combined that the thought, and even to some degree the mention of God at all, was cast aside, and other mundane and monetary issues were placed before God, and the image of God was sullied by our greed and expansion. We were searching for new lands, for new areas, for new riches, however we never searched within ourselves. Without first knowing and loving yourself in entirety, it is impossible to love another or even God.

God is again within you, and to love yourself and to know yourself is to love and know your Creator, known as God. My personal relationship is closer to God today than when I was forced to go to church every Sunday, and "be a good catholic." I found that discovering God and me at the same time is the only way to find the true self meaning of God and all that is.

Without your own firm beliefs and self-awareness you will never know the true God. The God that religions tell about varies highly amongst the majority of religions on the face of this planet. Spirituality is more the way to God than religion. Religion and "holy" wars have destroyed the true meaning and face of God in our Earth society today. Each religion has real substantial truth; however, no religion encompasses the entire meanings of God and spiritual evolution.

For me, religion has been destroyed, and personal beliefs and faith are the replacement in our spiritual revolution to our personal paths to our God. By "our God" I do truly mean God, as the only full God is every conscious person's perspective of God on the planet at this time, as well as throughout the entire Universe.

Q: Weston, who is God?

Weston: God isn't religion. God isn't a stern figure who punishes us for doing something bad. We punish ourselves enough without having to have God do it. People become afraid when they have had experiences that weren't good, or they don't let themselves have experiences just in case they screw up. Using the concept of an Almighty God just gives people an excuse not to be free inside or to accept that they have choices other than what they can see or experience.

Because we *are* perfection, we *are* God. "God" is a word that tries to define our source. That is impossible because our Source is an infinite field of energy that manifests as light. That light is inside of us, in every cell in our bodies, and we can draw from that.

When we pray, we are really calling to the light to tell it what we want or need. The light responds and reality changes. We have that light within us. It acts in response to everything that we do. It changes our reality based upon everything that we believe.

People personified God in order to have a deity that they could understand in human terms, but it is much greater than that. The most wonderful thing is that all of reality is enfolded within us. We are encoded with every imaginable possibility. All we have to do is imagine it and it becomes true. That is, if we believe it.

So the bottom line is that everything is a choice. Life, love, happiness, all of it. In order to address the God within us, the God that we are, we have to let go of our fears, breathe, and realize that those fears are unfounded—that we are of perfection and, therefore, we are perfection.

Q: Tristan?

Tristan: For me, God is light and energy, very loving and peaceful, and this energy is in everybody and every living thing.

Rhianna: God is the Creator of the whole Universe and something WAY more than a person. Our relationship to God is more than religion.

Q: Jasin, what about you? Who is God?

Jasin: God is everything. God is everything that did, does, and will ever exist. We are related by our soul—our soul is God.

Q: What about religion?

Jasin: There is no such thing as religion. They are not teaching you anything. You have to find out for yourself.

Joseph: I think that God is not a person, but the energy that surrounds us. I think that our relationship with God is the energy that gives us the strength we need to do what we need to do. To give us courage in our hearts. To bring us truth so that we can show His truth. I think that religion is a way of bringing Him into our lives. I think yes, religion is a way to relate to God, and I think that's all I have to say about that.

Scott: God is the one who created us here on Earth, but like on Montanui, they have a god which in all explanation there is the same identical thing. Basically, He is the creator of all life. He's something more.

Q: Is that relationship the same as religion or...?

Scott: It's definitely not the same as religion...but.... It's impossible to describe.

Q: Ahn, is God a person?

Ahn: God is definitely more than a person; God is everything, especially intense, unconditional love. We are sparks of God, so our relationship is tight—very connected. God, or All-That-Is, brings everything together, and religion seems to separate; so, to me, a relationship with God is not the same as religion.

Gabriel: God is something and nothing at the same time. God is a reflection of us. Anyone can believe in God as a reflection even if they do not believe in religions. God is not a person, energy, or light, but a feeling. God is very real and very alive. God is like those photo mosaic pictures. All of our souls together create the whole picture that makes up God. Each of our souls is in a certain part of the whole picture of God.

Q: How do you identify yourself with God?

Gabriel: The piece of my soul in God is in the part that is God's sense of humor. God is giving us signs all of the time. Our job is to find out where the signs are and what they are. God put us here to fight our greed and desires. We are always being called to our better selves. The God in me likes to hear people laugh. I feel God the most as I sleep and have the dream of being happy.

Q: What about Angels?

Gabriel: I feel the warmth of Angels everywhere. Angels are like a really good feeling in our spine, like the opposite of that scared tingle that can happen in your spine. I think the Angels are everywhere; there is nowhere they try to avoid.

Q: Lindsay, who is God?

Lindsay: God is us. God is love. God is whoever and whatever you want it to be. God is a person, because we are people, yet He is an entity just as much as we are. God is the weed in your yard that won't go away, that dog that gets scared in thunderstorms. God is your neighbor and your best friend. God is everywhere because love is everywhere.

God is in every religion in some way, shape, or form. God attends church on Sundays, celebrates Shabbat at sundown on Friday, and makes pilgrimages to Mecca. We are related to God because God is us. And let's face it, you can't get much more related than to yourself.

10

In order to die, first you must live.
Humanity is so afraid of dying that
often it sits paralyzed, unable to
put one foot in front of the other
in order to participate in the
very journey for which they came.

—Weston

DEATH IS...

What is death? Do we really die? Is that it, all there is? One life and then we are finished? Or is there more? Where do we go? Is there something next? Every religion, every philosophy, has a belief about death. Some even use the threat of death as a means to control others.

One thing is for sure: We live to die. Our bodies are on loan to us for the experience of life. Ultimately, there comes a time when we must leave those bodies behind. Through near-death experiences, we have learned or heard that certain things happen as we exit our earthly existence. There is a tunnel, and at the end of that tunnel is a bright light. We might see other people who we know or to whom we are related in this life. We might be escorted by a group of people or beings to wherever we go next.

Some say that we go through a review of our lives, feeling the experiences of everyone we encountered and with whom we interacted from their perspectives. That possibility can certainly give us an entirely new perspective about how we treat other people. Knowing that we go through a life review during which we experience everything another feels (for which we are directly responsible) gives us the knowing that we might just want to treat others a lot better than perhaps we have up to now.

Other things may happen too. This writer thinks of the dying process much like resurfacing from a deep scuba dive. As we come up from the depths, we must stop every once in a while and clear our ears, letting our bodies adjust to the change in pressue under the water.

Similar to diving, when we die, we rise back to our Source one level at a time, stopping to equalize and process what we have learned and experienced as our vibrations rise back to ethereal levels. We take time to equalize to the higher vibrations as we move outward from dense existence.

The kids remember being with God (whom most of them describe as energy or light), and carefully choosing their parents, the when's and how's, and other details of their coming reincarnation. Their stories are too often said by unrelated families and others not to be true. The children's rememberings often challenge the belief systems of adults and religious backgrounds; nevertheless, their stories are generally consistent and the details undeniably similar, even identical.

I wanted to know from these gifted beings what happens when we die? At the same time I didn't want to lead them in a specific direction, so I asked them this:

Q: What is dying? Where do we go?

Jude: Dying is just the next phase of our soul's existence. We go to the other side to a waiting-type area in the cosmos. We then proceed to the crystal city to review our lives in their entirety. It is similar to how I explained my out-of-body experience. I have been given insight in many forms and validation of those insights since my out-of-body experience, however.

One thing that I was clearly shown was that when you sit at the crystal city council of masters, you review *all* of your lives—not just this one. You review them in many different perspectives and through many different people's point of views—not just your own. Some people think that you only review this life in which you were conscious; however, I have been shown differently. It is as if all of your past, present, and future lives end at the same time, and the soul pulls them all to the crystal city for the review.

It is not necessarily your final review, as many will notice that they have unfinished lessons that they still need to learn using the emotions and five senses only offered through the human form; that is, when they are returned in another human vessel. The time frame for all of this is the confusing matter. It seems to take only seconds to review your lives; however, you fully review them in their entirety and from many perspectives, so the timelessness of the crystal city is a huge factor.

I have also been shown a different aspect of this journey. For some it takes time to realize that they are dead. They end up in the etheric realm and become what many call "spirits" or "ghosts." These souls are on a different journey before they end up in the crystal city. There were lessons they needed to learn that they did not fully go through because their lives for the most part were cut short. There are different stages that I was clearly shown in this matter.

They are similar to the psychological stages of death that are talked about in many college psychology courses and books about death. The first stage is the acceptance of death. The Spirit needs to realize that it is dead while in the present form. The second stage is the stage where the Spirit needs to learn how to be a Spirit, how to manipulate the energies around them, how to interact with other Spirits (and sometimes the living), and how to live as a Spirit.

The third stage is when they need to learn the lessons that they did not fully develop as a living human being. The fourth stage is the learning of the lessons that they have not learned. Many people call this "unfinished business." The final stage is the moving on after their lessons are finally completed, and this is when they go to the crystal city and review their lives.

The time frame for this is not something that I have been shown, as I do not view time as a linear concept. It could take anywhere from a minute to a couple hundred of years. After we review our lives there are many "jobs" that souls can undergo, from my understanding.

We can sometimes be given the choice to come back into human form, and at that time I sense that there is a type of waiting list that we sign up for. There are also other jobs that I know the soul can take on. There is an initiate master type of soul career, Guardian Angel career, and many others that exist that I am unaware of at this time. There are also other parts of the Universe that you may go to and be incarnated as another form of sentient being.

An example of that would be Nuevo, where I sense and feel my Soul Energy is from originally. There is a lot to experience in this Universe and galaxy, and we are able to fully experience it all on our own schedule. After the human death, you continue that schedule at your own pace, in your own time.

Weston: In order to die, first you must live. Humanity is so afraid of dying that often it sits paralyzed, unable to put one foot in front of the other in order to participate in the very journey for which they came.

Every aspect of life serves a purpose. Even the most minor things in life are of vital importance. Take bamboo for instance. It is both fragile and strong. The water nurtures the bamboo, and at the same time cleanses its environment and brings elements of peace. The richness, the tannin from the bamboo, contributes to the richness of the water so that it can continue to contribute to the nurturing of all that surrounds it. Even the insects are symbiotic with the plant's health and growth as they live in harmony with the plants, and the bamboo contributes to the well-being of the bugs by providing food and shelter.

But in all of that, the cycles continue and ultimately each has its death, and with that death the decaying remnants of what was feeds the very environment that brought it life, sustained that life. This has always been so. There needs to be no fear of death. It is a fact of living. In fact, death is part of the illusion. You don't die. You just continue to be part of an infinite cycle. In all of that, remember to *live*!

Tristan: We die because our physical bodies can't live forever. Then our spirits go to different solar systems to share what we have learned. We can also help the people on Earth.

Peter: I think that dying is the point in which the end of that life of one's self has been fulfilled. I think that we go on to be placed in another life.

Nathan: When we die, our spirit goes to heaven. Once, when I was big, I met a baby named Noah. He died and I saw his spirit go to heaven.

Rhianna: When our bodies die, our spirit can go to heaven; we can watch over and help people.

Jasin: We go back to our soul selves. We never actually do die. It's just a myth. We're actually dreaming right now. When we die, we wake up.

Joseph: Once we know that we have fulfilled our purpose, whatever we chose it to be, we go to where our choice is. I think we go and stay here or be reborn. You don't know where you're going to be because it comes from your heart. You let your heart decide where you want to go. I guess if you say you want to be physical again but your heart says you want to be Spirit, I guess it's just your heart's decision then.

Scott: Dying is when one's physical life is over, but their soul's life is not. Where you go...you get to choose. Everybody chooses where they want to go after dying.

Ahn: I look at dying being a wonderful experience, leaving the physical then being in the presence of my Angels, Spirit Guides, God/Source/All-That-Is.

Q: Scotty, what do you think happens when we die?

Scotty: I think we go up and to some other dimension or our home dimension and we assess what we did in our lives and whether or not we need to go back, or what we need to learn again, or we just be in the infinite knowing.

Q: Do you think that we chose to come here?

Scotty: Oh yeah! Most definitely.

Q: Do you think we had specific reasons for coming here? I mean individually do we think we had different reasons from one to the next?

Scotty: Oh yeah, I think each soul has an evolutional path they need to follow, different things they need to learn.

Like there are some people who are just disciplined from birth and there are some people who are just so lazy. My brother is so disciplined, and I am like, well, I will clean if I'm told, and I am starting to work on that. I'm starting to crack down on myself, like I need to hold my weight around the house. If you tell my brother to do something he is right on it. He works out every day, and he cleans, and I am just like, urgh!

Q: And so he is accomplishing different things in his life than you are? And that's okay.

Scotty: Yes. He has experiences and gifts in some places and so do I. He has gifts that I have and I have gifts that he has. He has gifts that I don't have and I have gifts that he doesn't have.

Q: And that's really okay because you are on different journeys.

Scotty: Right, completely different paths.

Gabriel: Truly dying is when we have lost our soul, but when our bodies die we just go to that place we have inside of ourselves.

Lindsay: Dying is a body term. Our bodies die. We do not. We just move on. We go back to where we started, at the Source, and sit around the table with our "people" discussing the next contract and new lessons that we want to learn.

11

It's time to stop and to understand
what the beings of light already know.
We are all one.

—Tristan

PERCEPTIONS
of WAR

In the beginning times, wars were fought for survival. Now they are fought for power, political gain, for money, religious beliefs, and for control of natural resources. Many are fought in the name of God.

Throughout my entire life, I have never understood why humanity kills each other, for any reason. To me, killing is inconceivable, life is sacred, and each life is part of a greater whole. In my perception, to kill anyone is like killing a part of yourself.

The simplicity of taking a life never ceases to amaze me. How one can be living one second, and the next, through an act of war, one no longer exists on Earth. Just like that. Over an idea or an ideal that isn't truth and isn't in the interest of the entirety, only in the interest of a few. I am saddened that we war amongst each other instead of supporting each other across the globe.

When I hear that tens of thousands of children across the globe die each day from malnutrition while others throw away excess food, it breaks my heart. When I see refugees shown in the evening news carrying what they can, including members of their own families who are too weak to walk, trudging aimlessly down roads which lead to imprisonment in refugee camps or worse, I am incensed. I am absolutely stunned that anyone would consider taking what they will at the expense of the lives and well-being of others. Others will cheer on the conflicts as if they were at a football game with one team winning. In war, no one really wins. There is a cost to everyone. To some more than others. This is the primitive and unevolved human experience.

How on Earth can humanity survive the destruction that has occurred and continues to occur between nations, amongst its people?

Interestingly, when I asked the children about this subject, many of them wouldn't even participate to answer the questions. At first I thought maybe this was just because they didn't know much about current events or even history. What I later realized was that by participating in this part of the book, they were giving war the power of reality. They didn't want to go there. The children are about love, about life, the very nature of the land and the water, of nature and peace in general. They did not want to bring anything negative into their worlds. Can't say that I blame them. And thank God they are our next generation!

Those who did answer did so thoughtfully and with great depth.

Q: How do you feel about war?

Grandma Chandra: Useless.

Q: How can we stop it?

Grandma Chandra: By electing officials who share our viewpoint.

Q: What are your feelings about war? How can we stop it?

Jasin: We can stop war if we just settle down. There would be no more wars, guns, canons, swords, no more war stuff. People are greedy and greed doesn't even exist. It is make believe. The answer to war is already inside you. The worst thing about war is that it still happens. I feel very sad that people like war.

When I asked my cat about war, he said, "I feel very hurt in my heart." He wants to go right in the middle of it to stop it. You'd have to go deep inside their heart and make it so they don't want to do it. Make it so they want to quit. Like—go deep into their heart with your soul and stop them.

Jude: The first impression that I received on this topic was the experiment the galaxy calls "Earth." What I have been shown was that there are various planets in the entire Universe. These various planets are inhabited by sentient beings that are comparable to humans; however, they have different physical structures and characteristics. It is much like what we have seen on *Star Trek* or in *Star Wars*. Each planet is inhabited by a race of these sentient beings; however, unlike Earth, they all reasonably look the same. Their physical characteristics are the same, but not their structures.

It would be as if there was a planet that is comprised of all the same-colored beings. There are some planets that have a varied spectrum of races; however what I was shown was that there were representative energies that were bundled together and sent away to make the Earth. These representative energies were not all from the same galaxies. They were from the different corners of the entire Universe.

With these energies there also came the home energies of the planets' beliefs, faith, and other aspects of the origination planets. To me, it is obvious why war sometimes breaks out. With all of the different entities that comprise our Guides and other beings that are around us, combined with the varying energies of the experiences of the souls that were sent from the different parts of the Universe, it would be hard to eliminate conflict. That was the essence of the experiment known as "Earth": to send out all of the energies of the Universe and represent them on a planet where they would see what would happen when all the energies collided.

All these energies including white, gray, and dark came to the area that is now our solar system and made the Earth and the other various planets that are contained within our system. When sentient beings began to populate the Earth, they were of different races and physical makeups due to the influence of the soul energies from their original planet of origination within our Universe. It's these various energies and influences that contribute to what we call war.

The dark energies were a big factor in the concept of war, as they manipulate and change the thoughts of some susceptible souls that are in human form. With the various energies and the introduction of the dark side, it was obvious to me that there are many opportunities for war. It was in the concept of that experiment that we would peacefully organize the planet; however, free will and the various energies and souls on the planet transformed the peaceful thinking into violence and darkness that are produced by wars.

The second thing is the division and combination of church and state. This is an age-old combination that does not mix. When you mix church and state, you are really, in essence, mixing money with faith and religion. This, as shown to me, was the downfall of the religious systems of the Earth for a very long time. It seemed to start with the explorations of the different continents of the Earth. The particular time periods that come to mind are the times of the Conquistadors, the Jesuits, and other faiths that conquered people by masking their dark energies of expansionism with religions. It was the constant push to find new land, and new monetary gains in the world that ripped faith from religions.

The conquering and destruction of the Mayan, Incan, and Aztec civilizations, as well as the Native American cultures and civilizations, began the age where church and state would be combined and the downfall of the human race.

It is the combination of these two theories and life energies that killed the true concept of being a human being on the planet Earth. It was their cultures that combined a way of life, monetary or barter systems, and religion in the perfect blending that would allow life to flow through them and their beliefs in peace and harmony.

Two more examples are the civilizations of Atlantis and Lemuria. These two civilizations were the same perfect blending that allowed them to prosper, until the third concept entered their lives.

The third concept was the concept of the "ego." The ego entered into the lives of the sentient beings. It was not the ego of the Mayans, Incans, or Aztecs that failed their civilizations. It was the egos of the conquering countries that aided in the war and destruction, as well as the invitation of the dark energies into places where they were unknown until that point. Atlantis is a perfect example of this theory.

From what I have seen in my own visions, as well as read about regarding the various concepts of Atlantis, there was a group or one person that decided to obtain the power of the crystals and the archives for his own uses. Ego was the introduction to the dark energies into the Atlantean civilization, and ultimately its downfall.

This can be paralleled to what is happening in the Middle East at this time. The "Holy Land," which is so sought after for its historical events, is under attack by various nations. The concept that they follow is that their religion is the only correct and 100% accurate religion on the planet and that portion of the planet known as the Holy Land is rightfully theirs.

There are many different religions and no one religion is the right religion on this planet. There are many aspects of varied religions that when added together create the Earth's religion; and in that spiritualistic religion, that is the one and true religion of Earth. This is also part of the first theory of the Earth experiment theory, as with the various energies came various faiths and ways of worship of the One Creator.

The "Holy Land" is not holy. There is nothing more or less special about that portion of the Earth than any other portion of the Earth except the events that took place there. It is the ego's attachments to that place, as well as oil, that make it a sought-after location. It is materialism, ego, religion, and the individual that create and bring war to the Earth. If we were to realize that we are our connection to God, and the Earth is holy, and it is in our differences that we should celebrate life, war would subside and we would enter the ascended state of peaceful living.

Only through self-realization of the God within each of us will war end. There is no simple answer to this since war has existed since the ages of Lemuria and Atlantis. There are many things that seem like the answer that are not. I know that the peace will come to the planet once we are all self-sustainable through our actions of everyday living. This includes our basic needs being met without the need of money. Water, food, and shelter being our necessities, being free for all the inhabitants of the Earth. These should never have have been compared to or combined with monetary gain.

The separation of church and state is also a factor. The government should never have been connected to the faith and religion of its people. The complete separation of money and religion, as well as religion and government needs to be addressed before the age of peace will come about.

What I have been shown is that a very large-scale Earth event will actually have to occur to wake up the peaceful way of living on the planet Earth. There will be hundreds, if not thousands, of deaths during this event; however, it will be necessary to the progression of the human race, as well as the Earth energies, to do a 360- and 60-degree turn around from money to peace.

Rhianna: War makes me sad, mad, and unhappy.

Q: Lindsay, what are your thoughts and feelings about war?

Lindsay: War happens when people are afraid. Fear only leads to death. Time will stop war. We are already moving towards a more peaceful existence, and though it may not seem that way, the old warring generations are dying out and new generations full of love, who are less fearful, are coming.

Weston: War is misuse of free will. Somehow I don't think that when free will was given it was meant for the destruction of life and lives. People often use free will for the misperception of gaining power. Really, that kind of power isn't truth at all. Power isn't gained by murder. It is gained by recognizing inner perfection and bringing that perfection into everything that you do.

A lot of wars are fought in the name of God. That is what happens time and time again in the Middle East. Everyone thinks that their God is the One God. The problem with that is that they are God and the reality that they are creating with their God selves is the direct opposite of who they really are. God is Love. We are God. We are Love. Every person in the world has feelings and fears, thoughts and perceptions, but what many don't have is the realization that they are everything that they seek. So they take from others what was never theirs. Maybe instead of taking guns to their neighbors they should take food and building supplies, freshwater and a new attitude. There is enough of everything on the planet for everyone if everyone would share their resources; there would be no desperation, and life on Earth would be an entirely different story.

Tristan: I think that war happens because people forget why they came here. You know, what their purpose is. We all have a reason for being here. God told me that I had to come because I had to teach people to love again because they forgot. Sometimes when I feel all the anger in the world, I forget what my purpose is and begin to get anger and act out. Then my mom and dad help me with my energy and then when I can calm down we talk about my purpose. So I think that this is what happens with leaders and all of the people they work with. They feel so much fear because they forget who they are and why they came to Earth. Then it just gets worse and worse because they are with each other all the time and continue to talk negatively about others and other countries. Then these people begin to act out on their words and the killings begin. They have been doing this over and over again in every life they have had on Earth. It's time to stop and to understand what the beings of light already know. We are all one.

12

Let's talk about harmony!

Let's talk about the earth and its existence.

For millions of years the world existed in one manifest form.

Now the world is changing.

—Nicholas

OUR GRAND CELEBRATION
THROUGH CO-CREATION
© BY NICHOLAS M. TSCHENSE, 10 YEARS

We are all here in this grand benediction
Yet we need to know to love without
affliction.
Crystal Children are here as a new generation
We like to bring love to this whole situation.
So when you ask us what's up for 2012?
The simple answer is a grand celebration.
Coming about through our co-creation.

2012 From *the* Children's Perspective

According to the Mayan calendar and pure scientific fact, our solar system, the Earth in particular, returns to its galactic center in December of the year 2012. As we fly through space in the direction of our core beginning, we enter the photon belt. As we do, we receive more light than humanity has received in the last 26,000 years.

We return to our galactic center every 26,000 years like clockwork. It has been stated by visionaries and scientists alike that these 26,000-year cycles often bring about Earth changes, such as extreme weather and earthquakes, as well as shifting of the poles of the Earth. What that means is that the Earth literally moves its position from upright, as we are accustomed, to a complete flip. The south becomes the north and visa versa. When a pole shift happens, the entirety of climate and electromagnetic influences are changed. Ice ages often occur, and the crust of the Earth moves in order to maintain the literal balance of the planet.

Because of these types of events, the people of our planet have had many new beginnings. At times, we did not survive at all, except for a few people. Those few were the new beginnings of humanity.

To me, 2012 is the beginning of a new age and the dawning of possibilities of greater tomorrows. Sure, there will be changes upon and within the Earth, but that has gone on since the dawn of creation. Let's face it. Who are we to believe that the Earth will stop its evolution just because we have chosen to inhabit her? But we can make a difference in how that evolution looks. We are participants in a living organism that is a greater whole. Every thought, every action, and, in fact, every bit of energy that we expend communicates universally and changes reality. We are that powerful. Imagine if we all got on the same page? We could change our experience and that of the Earth completely. Imagine.

For others, there is great speculation as to Earth changes that might occur in the year 2012 or in the time leading up to that year. Others believe that the event will bring upon us the end times prophesied in the Bible. For some reason, humanity seems to be obsessed with their doom.

To me, this is an inherent memory or set of memories that we carry within us on a cellular level that actually recalls energetically a time when all or most of humanity was destroyed. There is inherent fear that it will happen again.

Some feel that the event in 2012 will be a dimensional shift. To others, there is no awareness or belief that there will be an event or events.

Similar to Y2K and other previous events, is 2012 just hype? Or is there really something to it? Many of the kids absolutely would not answer this question. Was this because they didn't know or do know? Only time will tell! Those who did answer had definite perspectives.

Q: **What do you think about the changes coming in 2012? Are people making too big of a deal about this or are we really going to experience big changes? If we are, what kinds of changes do you see?**

Nicholas: Let's talk about harmony! Let's talk about the Earth and its existence. For millions of years the world existed in one manifest form.

Now the world is changing. By this I mean changing to a vibrational energy not experienced before. Now before you laugh, let me explain what I mean. The Earth is now experiencing a transition to lightness unlike the dense energy felt by the Earth thus far. We can know this as we make the connection between our own feelings of lightness in our body.

Since the Earth is a mirror of our beingness, we can predict a direct relationship in us as well. We need to listen to this change as it happens. Within this change is a note for us to pay attention to what is right. As we feel the shift from more dense matter to less dense matter, we must ask the questions, "What is the shift about? Can it be that simple? Can it be that through a shift in physical matter comes a shift in consciousness? Or is it the other way around?"

The reason I ask you to pay attention is to notice this change as we watch the shift to lightness. Through the very act of watching, we are creating more lightness.

May I suggest this relationship can bring us all closer to where we want to be?

Instead of creating focus on what seems disturbing, such as a lack of form in the way we want, whether it is a lack of peace, lack of love, lack of perfect order in nature, if we choose to focus on seeing these things the way we want to see them, then we shall create more love, more peace, and more perfect order in nature.

Q: Is the year 2012 important to humanity or our world? Are people making too much of 2012?

Grandma Chandra: Yes, it is a dimensional shift that humanity has been through before.

Jude: I want to start with the vision that I was shown of the beginning of the Earth. The Earth began and there were souls that were sent here from other planets that added to the energies and souls that were used in the creation of the Earth.

This was a type of galactic experiment to see if varied races that are represented across the galaxy could co-inhabit the new Earth without the ego or freewill getting in the way of peaceful habitation. The Earth began with no tilt in the axis. This meant that the sun hit evenly across the entire planet and seasonal changes were not as varied as they are today.

The Earth was mostly water, and then the first of the many 26,000 year cycles began. The universe that we are in rotates around the galaxy every 26,000 years. It is in the 26,000 year that it returns to the galactic center where it was created.

I have seen this center as a glowing field of electrons and protons and other atomic energies that look much like aurora borealis. As we approach the galactic center, there are many things that will occur to the physical and all other linked dimensions, and this includes every person's individual realities.

The Earth sends out internal reaction messages to the inhabitants on her surface. The major message that I have been receiving is to go away from water. All types of water. Rivers, seas, lakes, and especially oceans or coastlines. I was then shown a map of the United States a number of times. Each time the land shrunk more and more, and the water took over. The reason for this is because the excess energies that are being pushed out from the center of the Earth and the energies that are being attracted to us by the laws of attraction are huge in number.

There was a message that I got with this as well. It was that we need to utilize the excess energy in healing what we have done wrong to the planet the entire time that we have been here. It mostly targeted the Industrial Revolution as that is when we seriously began to abuse the Earth, our Mother.

In the map, Vermont, New Hampshire, and Maryland were cut off as the Connecticut River is a long, overdue fault line. The fault is going to shift and there is going to be a gap created where water will flood the lands around the Connecticut River. This will separate the previously mentioned states from the main area of the United States. Cape Cod is going to be underwater, as is much of Boston and central Massachusetts.

A lot of the East Coast is going to be underwater, as is Florida and parts of Texas and the other south eastern coast. The Mississippi River is going to overflow and fertilize the lands around it. This is much like what happens to the Tigris and other major rivers once a decade. This has not happened in a long while due to our intervention through man-made dams and water regulators and barriers. This flooding is going to create a very wide area of water in the center of the United States, which will only be crossable by sea-fairing vessels. There are, of course, going to be some areas of this divide that are crossable by lesser boats, and there are also going to be some spots that are totally impassable.

The area of the West Coast that I have seen involves California and Oregon mostly. There is going to be a deep section of Oregon that is turned into a large bay. The coast of California is going to have large numbers of quakes that will lead to a large length of the coastline falling off, but not disappearing. I have seen it comparable to what Baja, California, is now; however, it is the entire length of California. I am trying to do a map of what I have seen, as these are very vivid and in my reality accurate visions of what is to come.

There is a "safe zone" that I have been pulled to move to in the United States. That place that has been "calling" to me is Sedona, Arizona. I plan to move there when the calling is too much for me to withstand. I have seen a date around 2011. There will be many people that are moving to that area during this time as well, as this is a message that the Earth is sending out to the key individuals that will be helpful during the massive change that is going to happen.

The Gulf Stream is going to change as well and become more of a circular pattern. That will follow up the East Coast. It then turns toward Great Britain; however, it then turns south and follows to the coast of Africa and then turns toward South America and follows its coast. The circular pattern is shortened much more than it is now, so that the water that is circulating is getting warmer and warmer every year. This also comes from global warming and the increased melting of the polar ice caps.

I have seen a large comet that is going to miss the Earth in a few years. What happens to the Earth's axis tilt, and elliptical path around the sun, will change significantly. The tilt will lessen, and the Earth begins to wobble slightly. This creates wobbling of the elliptical path around the sun as well. This could affect us greatly in the magnetic fields of the Earth, as well as how close or far we are from the sun.

I was also shown that Mars at one time was in the position of where the Earth is now, and the Earth is where Venus is now. This vision showed me that Mars was once inhabited and full of life, as it is the positioning away from the sun that makes the miracle of life possible. Mars is too hot for life now, and the Earth will one day come too close to the sun. The comet will be a large part of decreasing the time frame of this gravitational pull on the Earth from the sun. Venus will one day be inhabited by sentient life and beings as well.

The thing that people can do to aid in the energy transverse is to meditate on positive change. Use the energy to cocreate with other light workers to create the Earth that we were meant to live on. It is through changing the mass consciousness's beliefs and faith into one that reflects your personal and individual reality, and what you would like to live on after this change. It is through the transmutation of Earth's excess energies that we will create our new Earth. If we do not use this energy, it will use us and most likely transform many more land areas to water or lava. There are going to be many earthquakes, volcanic eruptions, hurricanes, tornadoes, and other natural disasters that will occur as these approach. They will occur in areas that have never had frequent activity.

There will be tornadoes where there never have been before on the planet and in the United States. We need to use this energy to progress mankind and our souls, as well as the Earth and her as an entity. In this co-transmutation of positive change we will survive and prosper long after the change has occurred. We will have learned from our past and remembered all our lives to use the information within our soul memory to create the heaven that many religions speak of right here on Earth. We will all get along; however, we need all the positive meditations and thoughts using this excess energy as possible to cocreate and not stay silent and vulnerable!

Some of the better things that I have seen in visions are the creation of metaphysical schools that teach far beyond religion and much about the evolution and continued fine-tuning of the souls journey in the Universe.

There are key people that are awakening at this time and reclaiming all their past lives into this one. This is so that we may utilize all of our abilities from all of our lives in this conscious state so that we may aid in the greatest way in this change. This for most people happens through soul traveling during REM sleep states. That is how I began to be aware of my healing on a psychic level.

There is major change that is approaching us, and we are preparing in these travels that occur each night. I have been traveling with my consciousness to a place where there is a large circle of people present, and they do not look anything like a human being. There are so many different types that it is very hard to explain. We are all sitting in a circle and meditating and as we do we are actually talking telepathically and holding a sort of meeting at the same time.

The information that is being discussed and the actions that are being planned at these meetings are what I explained previously. There is much more that I am unable to remember in complete detail, however the basic message is that 3,500 feet above sea level now is going to be the average new sea level. That will be the coast. The other part of the message is that we can still change this situation into a positive, creative change rather than a destructive change.

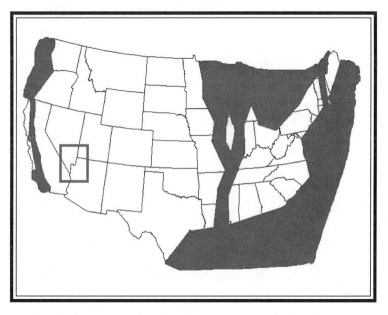

Predicted changes in the United States coast lines following 2012 by Jude DeCoff (© Jude DeCoff, 2007)

Weston: The coming times are of a cycle of consciousness and nature that has been repeated infinitely. Sure there will be changes on the planet. There are and will be continually changing patterns of weather and changes in magnetics and even of the position of the planet, but the most important changes will be how humanity as a whole embraces the reality of what is happening inside of them and in their external world.

People tend to act like sheep, following one person or group of persons and giving them all of their power. In the coming times, people need to get right from the inside out. Stop giving away their choices. People have become lazy, wanting someone else to take care of everything for them while they sit back and reap the benefits.

Everyone has the choice of creating a much different world. The way that the energies are setting up, there is the greatest possibility of entering into a completely new age of consciousness. Consciousness in not just awareness, it is also action. When you intentionally live according to universal law, and you are a living testament of greater choices, then you are contributing your highest and best to the totality of the One. Everyone is part of that One, so when anyone decides to become intentionally involved by acting in the same way that you want to be treated, the relationships amongst people will change. And when that changes, then relationships among nations will change. When that happens, the possibilities of universal peace begin to fall into place and the world has become Eden on Earth.

With the changes are going to come certain events that involve celestial bodies that will reshape the interrelations of multiple solar systems. This has happened before when influences change the orbit of a celestial body or bodies, and there are collisions of those celestial bodies with others. This is how the Kiper belt was formed. It is why our 10th planet now rotates around two suns.

There are always interrelations amongst the celestial bodies, and, similar to people, each celestial body has a personal space. When another celestial body comes into that personal space, the relationships amongst everything changes. When those relationships change, the actual vibrations of every level of reality change too. That is what will happen. The question is how many people are willing to live a conscious, purposeful, intentional life?

Rhianna: In 2012 we are going to be too dependant on technology to do things for us.

Jasin: No. It's not important. It doesn't even exist. We just made up some calculation. There is barely anything to it. Something has changed to where it isn't important.

Joseph: I see that each year, we will grow to learn more and more. I really don't think to far in the future; maybe tomorrow or the next day or week from now. I would rather live in the NOW than in the future because you need the experience from NOW to get to a better future.

Scott: I know one thing: technology will be more advanced than it is now, and so will human behavior. In my opinion, I don't think the world is completely ready for all the changes that are about to happen.

I see more advanced technology and weapons, and they are highly stolen from some great place where they have the most powerful weapons locked up inside. Many people are trying to break in and I see some prevailing. It's the only changes I see clearly.

Q: We were talking earlier about how things will shift. How does that look to you?

Scotty: Well. A lot like this: We used to have a creek down by our house and I would go and sit there and all of a sudden everything would be so clear, as if I have entered the fifth dimension, and I would look around and say, "Wow, everything is so different than when I first got here."

Q: Oh, when everything looks so crisp and new, and you can see every little detail?

Scotty: Yes, and the wind is perfectly timed and the grass seems to sway and dance in time, too.

Q: Everything is in sync.

Scotty: Yeah—the most amazing things have happened to me whenever I have done that. Like I was walking home after one of those experiences and ran into a whole family of screech owls. Another time two deer came running toward me and stopped, and I saw that it was a mom and her baby.

    When I see these animals I just quietly sit down and be with them, just be in their energy until they fly away. Then I get up and go home.

Lindsay: You know, I do not think it will be major chaotic disasters—I am not really sure if 2012 is even the right year. But I do know that shifts are coming, whether they are in forms of earthquakes, hurricanes, or if they are under the radar; if they are shifts in the way we think, they are slowing happening.

Tristan: I guess we will just have to wait and see....

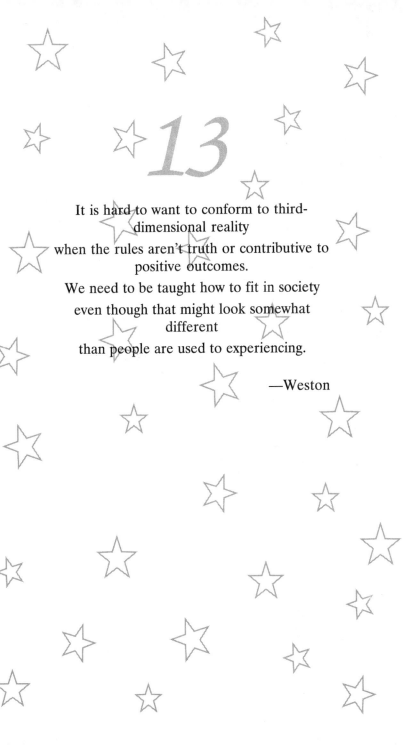

13

It is hard to want to conform to third-
dimensional reality
when the rules aren't truth or contributive to
positive outcomes.
We need to be taught how to fit in society
even though that might look somewhat
different
than people are used to experiencing.

—Weston

WHAT OUR CHILDREN NEED

In my previous book, *The Children of Now*, I addressed the subject of what our children need. This included environmental changes, such as smooth surfaces, colors, furniture, additions of nature and music, and other things that would allow kids to feel more comfortable, as they are often subject to aural (hearing) and visual overload. These types of overloads act much in the same way in the children's ability to focus as static does when it interferes on a radio program.

Other suggestions included diet changes and supplementation, changes in school curriculum, and social environments.

I also addressed that many, many of these children are being diagnosed errantly with attention deficit disorder (ADD), attention deficit hyperactive disorder (ADHD), and autism. In fact, the minds of these children, as well as their consciousness, do not work in the same manner than those of previous generations. In no way are these children able to learn or behave in linear formats. It is impossible because their

195

consciousness and their minds are holographic in their order-ing. They compartmentalize everything for current or later use. They don't miss a thing, even when they don't seem to be pay-ing attention.

These children aren't freaks of nature; they are part of a leap in human evolution. They are holographic thinkers. Imag-ine that instead of thinking in a straight line their minds work like infinite honeycombs, with each part of the honeycomb being able to store bits of information that can later be accessed. In truth, this is how these children think. In being, most of the children who are labeled as ADD and ADHD are similar to that. They appear to go about life at a whirlwind pace, seeming not to be paying attention, when in fact they are gathering in-formation faster than others can comprehend. Later, they draw on their observations for full understanding or perception. I have often been startled after observing these children in action at just how much they had taken in. When the children are treated as if they are different, they develop low self-esteem.

Autism is a different affectation. The electromagnetic energy fields in the bodies of these children are, shall we say, inflamed. This is caused by a variety of influences, such as mercury in their system, which is a highly conductive metallic liquid at room temperature, and, when heated, becomes a gas, such as what happens in the human body. This allows for the electromagnetic and electrical systems in the body to become hyper-functional. Because of this, consciousness, which is also energy, does not "seat" fully in the body or the brain. The children do not seem to be fully functional or present, but really, there is nothing wrong with them other than their con-sciousness is living multidimensionally.

Of course there are other reasons that the consciousness does not seat fully in the body, such as birth trauma or other trauma. I have worked with children (and even some adults) who actually died in the birth process or from a severe trauma, who were brought back either spontaneously or by the heroic efforts of others. In those cases, the consciousness did not seat fully because of the shock of returning to the body. In those cases it is as if the consciousness was on its way back to where it originated, and was suddenly jerked back into the body. As that occurred, the consciousness fragmented or did not make it all the way back in. (Similar affectations occur when someone is comatose. The consciousness is present on some level close to the body, but is not in the body enough to be responsive.)

The point is that our new generations are not necessarily dysfunctional, just differently functional. Not all of the children are diagnosed with ADD, ADHD, or Autism. And even those who are, probably are not. The children are more highly functional that we can wrap our minds around. And they have needs. They are so sensitive, subject to feelings and functioning that we do not understand, that we often abuse them without realizing it.

I wanted to give the kids an opportunity—from their inward experiences, as well as those events they have outwardly, in society and at home—to talk about what they need firsthand. I was interested to see that most of them spoke of "the children" in the third person, as if they were observers of their own experiences. Nicholas had spoken of "deep listening" in the foreword he wrote for *The Children of Now*. To be heard is the most common thread amongst the children. They feel as if they are not taken seriously. Okay kids—*we are listening*!

Here is what I asked:

Q: **Beyond deep listening, what do our special children need? What can we do to support them?**

Nicholas: I consider several things when I come to asking myself this question. First and foremost, are we being heard right now?

Second, how can caring members of the planet step forward to embrace and hold these children in their hearts? For this to happen, we develop a meeting place so we can meet our special children and truly experience their gifts from this cherished unfoldment. A synergy of love and action will bring us to a new place.

Third, our best and highest way of supporting these special children is to match their vibration through our harmonic resonance. By choosing to be in an aligned and authentic presence, we bring to the children energetic vibration that is like a coherent symphony to uplift the Earth's vibration. This is not unlike bees working in a hive to serve the queen bee by being aligned and authentic in their purpose. Their vibration oscillates to match the queen bee, and, in turn, the energetic vibration of the whole hive is being raised.

This is a metaphor for how we can be with these special children, yet all the while remembering that our first lesson is deep listening.

Grandma Chandra: Much love and allowing them to teach us what the next step is.

Jude: The children today that are coming into their lives with the memories of their soul's past need to be understood. Listening is not the end; there is much more that needs to be done. What would help is an interactive form of listening on an everyday basis. Especially when they come to you with these unknown sources of information.

Acceptance. I look all around me for acceptance, validation, and confirmation of what I am going through with my gifts, and it is difficult to find. The children are going to need the support and validation from the ones that are the nearest to their hearts in this life.

Knowledge. The children are going to acquire mystic knowledge from around the world and galaxy, and from sources that are seen and unseen by 3-D human eyes.

I have seen that there are "ushers" that are in the human form now. They are of my generation and have designed this human life to create outreach areas within which these gifted children can learn and grow.

I envision classrooms where the topics are psychic awareness and soul science. The world is in for a large quantity change and the children, if properly raised and nurtured, will be the ones to push humanity into its next phase.

The phase of love.

The children need these safe areas to be able to talk about these experiences and abilities without a fear of persecution or segregation of any type. Public awareness will be a huge factor in what I have seen as the Indigo "revolution." To me, it is more an evolution. There needs to be an integration of spiritual topics taught within the school systems if the children are to achieve full recognition and understanding of what Earth and humanity has to offer them as tools for the spiritual evolution of humanity.

The teachers that are going to be discovered are going to come from a pool of people around my generation. We are the ones that are to nurture and develop these special children. They need to not be kept silent, but urged to share their knowledge with the world in a judgment-free platform. When that happens, we can learn all that is possible from their universal heritage.

Weston: I am a very lucky guy because my family supports me completely, and that includes my other-worldly abilities that might frighten a lot of people. Children like us really need the support of everyone around us. Some of us can't take very good care of our physical selves, but other parts of us are outstanding. Since we are in the physical world to at least some degree, we need for people to believe in us. To know that we aren't some weird phenomenon or strange occurrence. We are everywhere (literally!). We know what you are thinking or feeling even before you do. That is because we are very psychically sensitive. We feel with our whole bodies, not just our inner feelings. Being one of the Children of Now means that difference is the new norm. We are different; not really, we are just reflections of who people are and what they can do. Humanity just forgot how precious they are and how capable they are once they really pay attention and aren't distracted by everyone else's ideas of reality.

What we need is support. It is hard to want to conform to third-dimensional reality when the rules aren't truth or contributive to positive outcomes. We need to be taught how to fit in society even though that might look somewhat different than people are used to experiencing. We need some sort of framework in which to thrive. People in lots of parts of the world have gotten away from family values, and that is not good, especially when there are children involved. Add to that the children who are sentinel beings, who feel and know everything all of the time, and that leads to a corrosive mix.

We also need schools where we can be who we are and become more comfortable in a learning environment. A lot of children like me are homeschooled, and in some ways that is great, but in other ways this necessity limits the parent who remains home to teach us. It also limits our socialization to a large degree.

More than anything we are not to be awed or put on a labeled pedestal. Just because we remember what we can do doesn't make us different. It is just time for a change. Humanity is on a fast track. It wasn't on a good one at that. With so many of us children entering the world the possibilities of change are escalated, and the potential for humanity to survive long term with a different set of values for the enhancement of all humanity are much greater.

Love us, nurture us, tell us the truth, teach us what we need to know to fit and to survive, love us some more, then love us some more....

Tristan: The most important thing for people to do to help children like me is for them to be honest about what they are feeling. That way they will express themselves in a good way. I am very sensitive, and when I am around people who are fearful and angry it is very difficult, because they are not expressing it in a good way. I would hope that these people can be honest with themselves, and that way they would be honest with others.

Christina: Help us to have our voices heard and trust us. When I am with like-minded people I feel accepted and loved for who I am, and I can really be myself. It's because I am not shushed or told to be quiet; I am listened to, and when someone can learn from me it makes me feel amazingly happy. It's one thing to be listened to, but it's another to be understood. I can listen to people and not hear a word they are saying, but I really try to *hear* everything they say. One thing people can do to support the children is not to hide them away, and let them be who they are.

Q: Scotty, so many of you children are so sensitive and thoughtful. Not only do you feel that way, but you act on that and I love that.

Scotty: Yes, but I definitely feel that there are some very angry children, like my sister. She is so angry.

Q: Do you feel like they came in that way or maybe they are just so wide open, so sensitive?

Scotty: Yes and they don't have a filter...

Q: And they just defend, defend, defend because they don't have the tools or the skills to deal with what they are feeling?

Scotty: You are right, yes. Like my sister. She is so intense with people and she doesn't realize how short she can be with them.

Q: How old is your sister?

Scotty: She is 11 now, but when she was younger, we had to pick her up and take her home from kindergarten because she threw such tantrums and was mean with her teacher. The teacher would tell my sister something and my sister would say that she didn't understand, so the teacher would just keep repeating herself. All the while my sister kept saying that she didn't understand. My sister was so frustrated.

Q: So the teacher just kept repeating herself and not speaking to your sister in a way that she could hear it?

Scotty: Right, and then my sister does the same thing. She will say something to us and we will say that we don't understand, and then she will keep repeating herself and finally explode with frustration. When she gets confused she locks up and she can't hear anything that you say. And then it's just gone from there. You just have to go let her read a book.

Q: Do people call your sister ADD?

Scotty: They call her all sorts of things like attention deficit, dyslexic—all sorts of things.

Q: So they are trying to put a label on her?

Scotty: Yes, definitely. And I don't think she needs that.

Q: A lot of times what is going on with these children is not that they are dysfunctional, they just aren't being communicated with in ways that they can embrace or that they can relate to because they are so hyper-aware. I notice that a lot of children, especially a lot of the younger ones like your sister, think compartmentally. You know, most people think in a straight line, one thing after another in a logical progression. A lot of children like you, and your sister, think holographically, in layered, compartmentalized formats. This way you can draw from lots of information at a time from all of those compartments all at once. It's like you can do 10 things at once. And keep up with all of it.

Scotty: The funny thing with me is that I have so much that I want to say, but my mouth can't keep up with me, so I will stutter. When I was little I had a stuttering problem because I had so many thoughts in my brain, and they were coming from all directions. My mouth wouldn't keep up.

I agree with you—a lot of people can't keep up with what is going on in us. Like my stepbrother—he is a math genius. At the beginning of every year he calculates everything he has to do to get a B in every class and do the very minimum of work. He does all of this with x's and variables and all of this stuff, but he can't tie his shoe. He can only go from point A to point B. A lot of people don't understand that life is not from point A to point B—it is Point Z to point A to point G to point T before you get to point B.

Q: That's how you children think...

Scotty: Yeah! We can compute the dimensional fractals out. That is second nature to me and I don't even think about it.

Q: Right, right, so that is why you are so far ahead of your teachers and what's next all of the time. Not that you are being a smart alec, that's just how your mind works.

Scotty: Exactly! Like Albert Einstein. He was horrible in school because he knew so much more than his teachers. He got bad grades in everything!

Q: I am seeing that a lot with the children that are in the public school systems, mixed with children that think in a linear format, who can't think outside of the box, and I don't think teachers really know what to do about this; that they aren't trained to deal with this kind of thinking.

I think in multiple tasks, like a wheel of activities that you could do one at a time or all at once. As long as you got to the bottom line within the set limits, don't you think that would be more comfortable?

Scotty: It would be so much easier because everybody expresses themselves so much differently, in different times and in different ways. For example, my sister just started going to this amazing school. Instead of giving the kids homework every night, they give it at the beginning of the month, and you can decide when you want to do it. As long as you do it.

Q: And how is that working?

Scotty: She loves it! She is doing so much better. The thing that makes me so sad about my sister is that she has had such a bad experience with learning. She associates learning with her confusion and her anger, and she just doesn't want to learn anymore. It's become hard for her to actually want to learn anything.

Q: Well it becomes a point of total frustration, and by the time that they get to be about 14, 15, or 16, they have some real problems. I am seeing a lot of that. I call those children the Transitional Kids. They see things and hear or feel things; they are very sensitive, but not consciously as some of the younger children. They begin to feel so negative about themselves that they get into self-destructive patterns, and often get into trouble or worse. They become sick at heart.

Some of the Transitional Kids get physically sick and no one can figure out what is wrong with them. I call this being "cosmically ill." It makes me so sad when all that was needed was for someone to say "I know what you mean, I know how you feel, it's real and it's ok," and give them an honest opening to express their feelings of lacking self-worth. But people aren't getting that. This whole situation concerns me deeply.

I have worked with some really damaged kids. They are so hurt by society and even their families. Not intentionally. Their families mean well, but don't have the awareness or the skills that are necessary to help. These kids don't fit in that mold. Your sister isn't one of these kids, but I sense that her frustration is similar.

Scotty: Yes.

Q: But what are her gifts?

Scotty: Oh my god, she can sculpt. It is amazing. She has dragon busts and heads that are so real.

Rhianna: Special children need for people not to tell them that they're weird. We need more places to meet other kids like us, to take classes, to have good food, and meet nice people.

Nathan: Children need kindness, peace, and love.

Jasin: We need to be treated with love. Help us practice how to live in love, peace, and harmony.

Joseph: I think that we should give them no fear of what they have. That's all I think.

Scott: Crystal and Indigo Children need a very positive atmosphere, surrounded by people who will support them, instead of saying, "Oh...it's nothing...its your imagination...you just saw a shadow, or...you're crazy!" which some people do. People that surround you and actually support you for being different instead of putting you down. It really helps.

Ahn: In my experience, my mother listened and respected me and that was very important. Other helpful attitudes are to allow us to go "outside the box," and to be encouraged to imagine and create. Children like us need a school that understands our sensitivities and allows for them. I'd like to see a school built out of crystals and with stone floors; no papers—just experiences (we absorb better if we can feel it). No immunizations or other fear-based thinking. Only high-vibration foods at lunch and thoughts for teaching would be there. Guidance in meditation, sound healing, yoga, finding the truth within, and so on would be so helpful.

Traveling is the BEST education. Programs that encourage living in other cultures, even for a little while, would be great for the children and the parents, too. Competition is of a lower vibration, so I feel it shouldn't be in our school system. I see schooling for kids like me as partnering with the teachers and a feeling of family at the school. The wisdom within each child would be acknowledged and appreciated.

(Scotty's viewpoints took a specific turn. He was most concerned about the type of education he and other children are receiving:)

Q: So what would you say to the schools of the world? This is your chance. You could say: "Schools of the world, teach us what we need...that we are different than the kids who came before us, we don't feel the way that you want to teach, we don't hear the way you want to teach it, and we know more." What would you say?

Scotty: I would say teach us stuff we can actually use. Because we are learning stuff we are never using. We don't use inverse functional equalities, or the information about some of those boring old people we read about. We don't use a lot of what you tell us.

Teach us how to balance a checkbook, how to go into the woods and build a house. Teach us how to be sustainable. Teach us how to actually use the stuff that we are learning. Because, they teach us how to learn it, but not why we learn it.

Q: So, teach in a way that it applies.

Scotty: So it applies! Because isn't that the point of learning? Why learn it if you aren't ever going to use it.

Q: Sure. It's taught by rote, that you just have to know it and you aren't allowed to ask why, that those are just the rules. So if you were learning in an environment where you learned how to apply, what it all means and what it is for, then you have an idea, and it's a lot more interesting that way.

Scotty: Right. One of the only things that I can think of that I have actually used since I started school is that, in chemistry, they taught us density weights of wood, and I think this is so great because I find all of these amazing sticks and branches and I don't know how to identify them because they are worn by weather and there aren't any identifying features....

Q: So you are able to identify them by their density?

Scotty: Sure. I can cut a piece off and I can go look up all of the medicinal or magical properties of the wood, and I can have samples of wood that I have already identified and measure their densities and then measure the densities of the unknown sample and know what kind of wood it is. So I can use that. It's the one thing I have been able to actually use from my chemistry class.

Q: That's exciting because you can apply that to your entire environment....

Scotty: Yeah and I can identify plants the same way. Take a known sample and compare the density it is an unknown sample and voila!

Q: How does the environment in school feel to you?

Scotty: My school is definitely an exception because we have the most amazing teachers. Like my English teacher last year had the most amazing principles. Like, if we had a 15-page essay to write, he would write one too, and then we would look at his. He would always sit equal to us. And he never sat at a desk. He would sit at a round table, and we weren't allowed to raise our hands because that made him seem superior, and that isn't how it is supposed to be. He had the most amazing perspectives that you can apply to life and judge his, too. And he would say, "Well that is a really good point." He really inspired me. And I think that a teacher's one and only job, their one and only job, is to inspire. To inspire the kids about learning the subject, because if you inspire them they are going to want to learn. And he definitely inspired us.

Q: That is a fantastic point. Even my own experience in school was that people made us feel less so that they could act as if they knew more, and that whole paradigm has shifted because the kids these days know so much more.

You said something to me earlier about how you are always light-years ahead of what the teachers are doing. Do you want to talk about that now?

Scotty: Yeah, for example, when I was in the fourth grade, the teacher in my Waldorf school put hieroglyphs on the blackboard, and I was like, I think I know what that says, and so she gave me an alphabet that I memorized in about a half an hour. I was starting to write it and it was hieroglyphics. Simple hieroglyphics—but I started to interpret things and it was ancient Egyptian, and I got a lot of it right. So it's that kind of stuff, like somewhere inside of me I already know these things.

Q: So you have a memory inside of you....

Scotty: Right.

Q: What about the physical environment you are in, the general school environment—you know, the colors, the furniture? Is there anything that you could suggest that would make someone as sensitive as you more comfortable?

Scotty: Most definitely. Like in Santa Barbara I went to a school with more than 3,000 kids. It was the desk, the walls, white tile, and you had this huge empty room with boring posters on the wall and other things, and you walk in the room and you are already bored. It feels empty and soulless. Soullessness. I can't stand that. My school now is better; we have colored walls. Wooowww. Woooooo...*That's exciting.*

Q: Well that is a big step for an institution.

Scotty: In my current school we actually have carpets, and there is one room where we have couches. In my English teacher's room we had round tables and cool posters on the walls, and posters of bands...

Q: So your teacher created a familiar environment for you.

Scotty: A room that actually has some soul in it. It's not just this empty white room where you feel like you are in an insane asylum.

Q: Doing your time.

Scotty: Yeah, doing your time. Actually, that is what a lot of school feels like. And everybody counts the time they have to be in school.

Q: Like let's watch the clock that is right over the teacher's head.

Scotty: That's right. We only have three more years, only two days until school's out...

Q: Because it's hard to be there...

Scotty: Right.

Q: I know that generationally that has been true. That every child in school has felt that way and, well, there are some who live it and that is great. But overall, the general attitude is that they can't wait to get out. To me, it's about creating an environment that is conducive to not only the humanity of the children, but the sensitivities coming in, children like you, all of that expansiveness, you know, the colors and shapes, the way the furniture is arranged and the whole room is laid out, you know, cleanness of the environment is so important. Less chaos. Getting rid of the visual chaos, having meaningful things and softening with live things, plants.

Scotty: Yeah that is what I love. Then if you get bored you can talk to the plants the whole time.

Q: Do they talk back?

Scotty: Yeah they definitely talk back.

Q: What do you talk about?

Scotty: Anything, anything, they know a lot about dimensions. You can ask them for their names, what's in their soil, what they like.

Q: Have you ever talked to any of the trees that have been around for hundreds of years?

Scotty: That is an amazing experience. They can tell you everything that they have seen since they were little, teeny saplings. They are so much fun, kind of like if only walls could talk.

Q: So what types of things do you get communicated in a situation like that?

Scotty: Well it depends. Sometimes the trees are really cryptic and sometimes it is just straight out. It's a lot like in the deaf society; I had a deaf teacher, so I took sign language and became fluent in it. I love how simple it is, like "You look fat today, are you pregnant?" I love the simplicity of that because usually people are like, "Oh, no! Don't tell her she has something in her teeth," and things get complicated or we just beat around the bush.

Q: That's an excellent point because when we talk with the plants and the trees, they communicate very cleanly and with no agenda. I don't think people realize that these things can really communicate with us.

Gabriel: They need to know what is going on in this world. Then need to have their hearts, minds, and bodies fed good nourishment, so they can be part of the solution.

Lindsay: Accept them. Forget the standard. Whether your child loves football, or just wants to study aliens. Whatever their choices are in life as long as it harms no one, support them. I see many parents trying to push their children in certain directions (normally the wrong ones), simply because that's where they think their child should be. The deep listening will help, but you have to work at understanding what you hear and doing something about it. You can share your learned knowledge with your children, hoping that they will make good decisions. Chances are if you support and love them, they will. Acceptance and love will be the key to the new generation's future.

14

If everyone would realize that
they really are creating the world that they
are living in,
it would change everything.

—Christina

When Darkness Knocks
By Jude DeCoff
(©Jude DeCoff 2007)

As you sit upon your chair
Wondering, Wondering, Where oh Where
The Guide, The Prophet, The King and Pauper
Each Life you lived you will remember
When time is right as there is all but none
You will see your fate in the stars above
The message, the vision, the light within
Will show you your path to the shining destined
Your moment in life you will see
The path as clear as the line of the Bee
With wings of gossamer and Fey the light to be
You fly away home with love, and an offering
of honey candy
The astral realm holds many surprises
The mermaids, the fairies, and the energy
that rises
You can see through the veil and through your
own blockage
Your clear soul with heavy karmic rockage
Like the chair with bows on the bottom
touching floor
You nestle your head in the bosom of mother
evermore
She loves, She holds, She caresses, and cares
She judges not fore she does not dare
To hate and hurt is not the way
Love thine self and you will succeed this day!

214

CHANGING *the* COURSE *of* HUMANITY

In nearly every nation on Earth, there is concern about the direction in which humanity is headed. Some think that we are on a path of self-destruction and that we are devastating our planet, the lifeblood of our human existence, by tapping out our natural resources, polluting the air, the water, and the land, and by our general disregard for the planet on which we live.

Humanity, in many respects, has become needful, directionless, complacent, and afraid to act unless some catalyst or challenge faces us directly. Rather than act directly, people will say that "they" can take care of it. The problem is that there is no "they," only a world of "us."

We are soaking up the resources of our planet. Some people are making a fortune on these resources, while others are paying a fortune just to use them. Overall, the whole situation is out of control.

For example, near the North Pole, the glaciers are currently melting. That glacial melting could, and will, ultimately cause global flooding of biblical proportions. Coast lines will have to be redrawn as a result. A very real possibility exists that people will lose their homes and their lives. Instead of governments doing what they can to find a cure for the problem, they are racing to claim more natural gas and petroleum resources in the areas that weren't previously accessible.

With the threat of global warming, of climate changes, Earth changes, drought, food shortages, and the lack of available or affordable healthcare, perhaps it is time for us to take a good look in the mirror.

Children always seem to have wonderfully innocent perspectives that contain truth in every morsel. Are our children aware of what is happening in our world? To find out how they felt about all of this, I asked them one simple question:

Q: **What will it take for humanity to change our current direction?**

And they were amazing:

Nicholas: Now as we are gathering and paying attention to the Crystal Children and ourselves, the Earth is listening and feeling fond love for us. As we continue to exchange like this, our planet Earth becomes excited and *much of the damage can be reversed*. This can be achieved through higher vibrational energy such as actual mass prayer and meditation on love, for our planet Earth.

(Grandma Chandra speaks of the polarization amongst people and energy harmonics on a more universal scale....The spirals of which she speaks are actually polarizations of energies, high and low frequencies, light and dark...)

Grandma Chandra: Many people have already changed direction; there are approximately 4 billion people that are choosing to participate in the new energetic shift of 777. There are two spirals of energy: one attached to the Third Dimension where we see more crime, war, torture, and so on, and the new spiritual spiral that many people have embraced. Both spirals are coming to their own conclusion.

Jude: The only way to change where humanity is going at this point is for a love vibration to fill our awareness and personal self-discovery to replace religion. Spirituality is the Earth's primary religion.

There is no religion that is going to lead to anything other than concerns of money and expansion. Holy wars need to cease. Nothing but love should be taken in the name of God. Through enlightenment, teaching of old, new, and present knowledge, and the human race joining together as one Earth race will things ever change.

We need to stop living out of our fears and live through our visions of light and love. For things to get better, increasing change needs to happen in an increased manner over the next few years.

We also need to harness the Earth's and Universe's excess energies. If we do not combine this with new views of each other, the energies will bombard the Earth through natural disasters and fears.

People thinking that they know God and themselves, and placing God's name and essence on war or suicide bombings, do not know God. They do not know themselves, and they do not search deep enough to find either themselves or God. They take the easy way out and follow like a heard of cattle following a bell. They do not take the challenging path of finding themselves and setting forth their beliefs in their society, especially when their beliefs do not match the majority around them. Only through perseverance, inner devotion, and finding ourselves and our life purpose will we ever truly find God. Then and only then will the world change for the better. There needs to be a large mass awakening and self-empowerment across the Earth that needs to occur before societal change will manifest.

Q: Jude, how can we do this?

Jude: Each of us needs to take into account that we make and change our own reality with our thought processes. Once we realize our internal reality creation process, then we can change our reality for the better. We will discover that we are in a cocreation process known as *life* that is hand-in-hand with the Creator known as God.

We have to undergo oneness and responsibility in self-reality before large amounts of change will manifest. If we do not change, there are many things that I have foreseen that involve natural disasters, large-scale religious wars, uprisings among the lower-class people that are in the lower income range, and many people losing their lives for a cause that do not reflect the Earth or God in any shape or form.

Reality manifestation and change are not easy. Many steps need to be taken to learn the process; however that is the true way of living and cocreating with the ultimate Creator.

Q: Weston, what can we do to change the direction that humanity is headed?

Weston: People have lost their senses of humor. Me, I laugh a lot. I love to pop into people's heads and make them laugh. The whole world is much too serious. People are so caught up in who is right and who is wrong and whose god is the real and only god that they have forgotten that there is only One and that one is all of us.

When you look at the world from above you can see that there are no lines at all, and yet all throughout human history wars have been fought over imaginary lines. That is because people can't seem to acknowledge their differences. Different skin, different cultures or beliefs, difference, difference. The truth is that when you look beyond all of that what you find are people who need, people who feel...people. Not enemies, not evil, but reflections of God.

There are people who are hungry and have nothing but the dirt on which they sleep, and even that isn't theirs. They and their children are starving and dying of preventable diseases while others hoard things and don't even think of anyone else. No one should ever go without what they need. *No one*.

If the basic human needs were met for everyone, if a coalition of people was formed in order to govern the balances, if everyone is the world were treated equally, that would be a great start toward overall change. What I am saying is that we need to move to a One World situation instead of living the fantasy that everyone has boundaries, and that changes are inside.

It should be okay and acceptable that people have different cultures. It is not okay for them to war over those differences in belief.

People sit around in complacency and imagine that "they" will fix things. "They" is all of us, and yet the majority of people don't act. They just go about their comfortable lives without regard to everything else.

More concern and action need to be taken in relation to the Earth. There are poisons going into the planet in the form of toxic chemicals and drugs that are changing relationships throughout the food chain. That changes how our food works in our bodies. It also changes what is safe and what is not. The animals are being affected too. A lot of the animals are dying. There are species that will never appear on the Earth again and that is sad. It can happen to humanity if everyone doesn't start to do their part.

The truth is that our preceding generations haven't left us a very healthy environment to grow up in; our families and people in current generations have made it even worse.

The resources of our planet are being used up and no one is making more. We only have one planet and we aren't taking care of it. People are destroying the balance of our ecosystem to a point when the damage will be irreversible. We have to put back what we take.

With all of those changes going on, planet Earth is dying. If she does she will take everyone with her, and it will be our fault for not acting. Not caring and not seeing what is right in front of us. If humanity is going to change direction everyone has to open their eyes and see what is really happening and do their part. It is possible and there is still time, but not much.

Tristan: I think that it is important for us to know how we are feeling inside. If we are feeling bad, we could talk about it with someone instead of acting out the angry feelings to others. Then we can feel the love inside.

Peter: More love, less hate, less fighting, more hugging.

Christina: If everyone would realize that they really are creating the world that they are living in, it would change everything. If someone says, "the world is a horrible place," then that is what they create for themselves and the world. But when you flip that around and say, "this world is beautiful and exciting," that is what you are creating.

Rhianna: Humanity needs to listen to the Angels and the Spirits around us. I want people to take care of the Earth; don't use it as a giant trash can! Also, listen to our Spirit Guides.

Nathan: Our world needs more peace and love.

Jasin: The answer to everything is love. Live your dream. Love your life. Love. Love. Love. Love. Love. Never stop.

Joseph: It will take each individual mind to change its head and send unconditional love to all people and help. I don't know what it will take or what will happen. I think it's the individual mind…each individual mind can work as a group to send unconditional love to everybody. I think we just hadn't tried that. I don't think we've done that yet. That may just be it.

Scott: Some people believe that something can change it. I do believe that something can change. It can change how we are right now. But what can change it…that I have no clue.

Ahn: Choice, willingness, focus with intention, and unconditional love is what it will take for humanity to change our current direction.

Q: How do you see the world changing to be a better place?

Scotty: I haven't figured that out yet.

Q: Okay. But as a visionary, because you are a visionary, what would you say we need to change in our world?

Scotty: I think that we need to acknowledge the other side of life. You need to not be so disconnected with yourself and not think that everything is materialistic. The American Dream is to have the blonde wife with the BMW, but there's definitely a lot more to life.

Q: So it's about becoming more in touch with ourselves, self-fulfilled rather than the external stuff?

Scotty: Yes, right. Know thyself and you know the Universe. That is such a great thing because if you know yourself, you can combat anything that comes at you, and anybody can call you a name or something like that and it won't really matter because you know who you are. It's kind of like water going over a rock. If you know yourself, you can be a really strong rock.

Q: Who are you Scotty?

Scotty: I am definitely a strong rock.

Q: So you think that by discovering what is inside of ourselves, that that would lead to a different kind of world?

Scotty: Yes. I am really trying to get to know myself so that I can do things in the future and not really break down. After you know yourself, it's like the pebbles that make the little ripples that expand throughout the entire lake. You've got to keep throwing all of those little pebbles in until one day you thrown a huge boulder in and the whole lake changes.

Q: We don't really know how we touch people or the world by every little thing that we do.

Scotty: Right.

Q: Every moment that we are counts, and I think that is what you are saying. Making positive actions, then everything can change.

Scotty: Right and if everybody stands by the lake and throws a pebble in it once, the lake can change so much. All of those people who have changed the world. Ghandi started out by just burning little papers, and he changed an entire country. He changed an entire planet.

Q: Lindsay, what is it going to take for humanity to make the changes we need to change our direction?

Lindsay: Time.

15

Black, white, or purple; gay or straight; male or female;
fast-food employee or Ivy League lawyer;
it doesn't matter.
What matters is love.
Because if we can't learn to love, what's the point?

—Lindsay

☆☆☆

Find your spirit.
Ask yourself what is important.
Really.
Be that.

—Weston

INSPIRATION FOR WHEN
THINGS ARE NOT GOING WELL
BY JUDE DECOFF
(©JUDE DECOFF 2007)

When life is going against your plans
Remember that God holds your hands
When things are dark and dreary grey
Ask your Soul from your Heart to Stay
There are lessons that you will learn on your way
Have faith, believe, and begin to pray
He hears you each and every time
You use his names in asking the Divine
He is there inside you within Your Soul
So relax, just breathe, and let it all go!

MESSAGES *for* OUR WORLD

Do you ever wish you could tell the world your thoughts, your feelings, the ideas that you have that you think no one has thought of? Do you ever wish that you had a chance to be heard in a widespread fashion? I can't begin to name the number of times that has happened to me.

Most children don't sit around trying to shout to the world. They are children who like to play and don't worry about too much unless it's about their allowance or if Billy can spend the night. The Children of Now worry about our world on very deep levels. In fact, they often tell us their thoughts and feelings, but we don't hear them. I really wanted to hear what the Children of Now have to say.

Having talked with so many of these children by now, I wondered what *would* our children say if they were asked? How do *they* see what is happening within humanity, our planet, our future? What do they observe that we need to change? How can our children, who are quickly evolving as beings of light, contribute to our awareness, to our perceptions of the true state of our world, and to humanity, when so many people are totally oblivious to what is really happening to us?

What would our children say if given the opportunity? Let's find out. Some of the children chose to contribute other input in addition to the basic question, so I have included some of those ideas as well. Will we hear them on a soul level, or will we think how profound they are, how cute, and go on about our business? I leave this choice to each of you. But I do ask that you read with the ears of your hearts. Here is the general question I asked them:

Q: What is the greatest message you have for the people of our world?

Nicholas: My greatest message for humanity is really simple: learn to listen to your heart. As simple as this sounds, it still asks much of us. In my own experience, I have found that when I listen to my heart, I am never guided wrong. Our hearts are the abode for every emotion, humble or not so humble. Our infinite soul energy resides in our hearts. This is the testimony of all our experiences throughout time. As we awaken to our heart center, we learn to live with grand love. There is a feeling that swells on the inside and continues to swell until we feel it overflowing with joy. This is how we know we are in our heart center. We are being asked to invite all ranges of emotion so that we can go into our heart center more.

Q: Nicholas, why is there poverty and suffering in the world?

Nicholas: I believe there is poverty and suffering in the world due to a gross error that humankind is making. This gross error is about thinking in terms of *lack*. Since there is a percentage of the population who gain greater wealth based on thoughts driven from fear, there is a tendency to consume more for themselves.

The result is what we call "poverty." This poverty is not so much due to impoverished thinking, as much as greed thinking. Replace this greed thinking with unconditional love, and their *lack* will surely diminish.

Jude: There is a large shift that is happening very shortly in the world. From what I have seen there are going to be many natural disasters and destruction; however, there will also be human survivors all over the new world. There are many things that we need to do to prepare ourselves for this event. Shows and documentaries are appearing all over the mass media that talk about global warming and flooding and mass destruction.

Please do not buy into the negative aspects and thoughts that these influences bring up in the human psyche. We need to take the excess energy that is being bombarded onto this planet and use it to heal her! Keep our thoughts positive in nature and love! We need to nurture each other and send healing and love energies to the places in the planet that are highly negative in the present time. Even thinking about positive things happening in places that you have never been sends a positive chain of events out into the Universe so that our Creator can manifest them along with our own personal manifestation energies.

We are part of Creator. We have the ability to save the Earth with our everyday thoughts and actions by thinking about negative happenings and then releasing them to the Universe with the intent of recycling them into positive events. Please do not feed into the negativity and let in the light and positive energies of the Source, the Creator, God, the Divine. Flow and shine each and every day. Be kind, loving, compassionate, and stop the mundane living of silence that we have been plowing through every day. Be interactive within your reality and cocreate with God the world that you want your children's children's children to develop and live in. Live life through and with LOVE.

Weston: Humanity must return to love. The world is filled with drama, fear, anger, and conflict. Change is necessary for the greater good of humanity. Change is resisted because human beings do not remember beyond their current lives, which are filled with massive information input and justification of practically everything they do. Humanity must remember beyond the illusion, that the vitality of life is not what it seems. They must let go of fear because the truth is far simpler. That fear leads to the lack of change. The unknown is beyond the known, and the fear of the unknown is beyond reason.

The lands of the Earth display the inner existence of humanity with all of the colors of joy and the unfettered spirit, and the desolation of a defeated heart. As the rivers flow, so does life. Then there is nonmovement, such as boulders on a mountain. Many people do not move in their lives. Lack of movement in life is sadness. Life is to be embraced and exchanged with all other life forms. The colors of life are not to be tempered by perceptions, only expanded in their resonance by exhilaration of spirit.

Compare yourselves to the animals, to those that scavenge, yet are their true selves. They have no fear, only the will to survive. They have the freedom of their basic natures, innocence by virtue of existence.

Those animals that are spoiled of their true nature don't remember their wildness except in their dreams. They fear many things because they have no experience. People are like that. Wanting to be spoiled, becoming too comfortable in their safe places, having, owning things, but not having any knowledge about life in general. They have forgotten their wildness, their innocence.

Innocence is found in the light of love, of grace. Humans become lost within and have embarrassment to display their grace as they would be embarrassed by the response of others. The truth is that others would respond in like manner, and their love, their grace, would shine even more brightly.

Diligence is the key. To always be aware of how you feel, what you are really experiencing, not the illusion. For the most part humanity has become so caught up in the illusion that they don't remember their true selves. Stop listening to what others say. Listen within. The answers are there. Being human is temporary, so all of those everyday worries don't mean anything in the overall picture of things. The spirit is forever. And that's what really matters. Find your spirit. Ask yourself what is important, really. Be that.

There is much hope but little faith in this world on Earth. Faith and hope are two completely different energies of feeling and thinking. Hope implies failure. Faith exemplifies the expectation of success. More, faith is what creates life when there is little hope of it.

Humanity has too many boundaries, particularly of needing to feel aside, alone in the journey, special or important. The truth is everyone is perfect. There is Joy in Oneness, to the joy of being whole. No one thing can exist without the other.

Tristan: I would like to tell people to find the love inside of them and share that with everyone and every living thing they meet. This is all God wants.

Peter: I think that would be that you should be grateful for the life God has given you and that you should be helpful when it comes to the children of God.

Rhianna: I want people to take care of the Earth; don't use it as a giant trash can! Also, listen to our Spirit Guides.

Jasin: They need to stop cutting down all the trees because when they are all gone we won't exist anymore.

Q: Do you mean everything, like we didn't even exist?

Jasin: Yes, and we'll have to start all over again, in another form.

Joseph: Hope...hope! Never lose hope, basically. With a little hope, you look on the bright side and you learn how you want to fulfill your purpose. If you just let your life run by, you just decided your purpose. So you should never lose hope.

Scott: The message I would give is to stop fighting and act as united as you claim to be. Leaders claim to be united: "We are all united. Now I declare war on you." That's basically it.

Ahn: All the answers for you personally are always within. We are powerful beyond measure; own that power, treasure it for your heart, soul, and your being. Keys I use are to focus on what's light; "desire" rather than "want"; do your best, expecting the best; and HAVE FUN!

Q: If you could say something to our readers right now, what would you tell them so that they know it's okay.

Scotty: I would probably say that everything *is* okay. Trust and love life. Because everything is perfect, and once you hit the bottom the only way to go is up...I mean everything has perfect timing and you are here to experience these things. For your own soul, you needed these things, to experience them and work through them. I believe in experiencing emotions 100 percent.

Q: Do you think we make mistakes?

Scotty: No, no; I really don't. I think that everything is perfect and maybe you were meant to learn a lesson or maybe you did this so that something else could happen. I have had so many experiences where I said, "Dammit, why did I do that?," and then I ran into the most amazing person, or something else perfect happens.

Q: Isn't it amazing how something you think was a real screwup can take you to the most miraculous event or experience?

Scotty: Like moving here, I was so deeply upset about moving for the sixth time. I was so in love with California, and I look back now and I am so happy that I moved here because I would have been a completely different person if I had stayed in Santa Barbara. I wouldn't have met so many of the people who have changed my life. I would have just stayed in what looks to me like a superficial life. There, I had extremes of being very social or not social at all. Here, life is very spiritual.

Q: These days there is so much input; there's TV, video games, movies. You watch TV and there are commercials on the screen and all of that input desensitizes people, so we can't find the feelings that are inside of us. We can't find that joy; we get numb, and we aren't even able to identify how we feel...

Scotty: Right. I just eliminate TV from my life. In fact we don't even have it in our hose anymore. And if I am somewhere and see it, I am just so overwhelmed by the commercials and how they are talking too fast and I can't stand it. I really think that TV and video games (and I used to play a lot of them) is kind of like a waste of life. Why, through the TV, live somebody else's life? Or why, through the video games, create a new life that doesn't exist when you could be living your own?

Q: Wow, that's powerful.

Scotty: That's what my main vision is, is that if you watch soap operas through someone else's turmoil, you can work through it with them, which is great for some people, but instead of working on their lives, you could be working on your own. Or like the online video games where you can create your own characters, invent an identity. Why work on that when you could be creating your own life?

Q: When you are creating a character like that, it's kind of like making a mirror of yourself, but it's out there in front of you. It's not real. It's hard to touch real soulful values.

Scotty: Well I think that we should develop our own lives instead of trying to live someone else's that doesn't even exist. You could be using that time to experience yourself, see a deer, read a book, experience nature....

Q: Touch reality...

Scotty: Yes. Touch reality.

Q: My sense is that touching reality brings us back to whom we are, and I mean by touching reality to use all of our senses. We have them. All of those things that are coming at us are teaching us that what we do have isn't important and they aren't even what is real. So it is about getting past those illusions and getting back to the simple things.

Scotty: Yes, simplifying things. In my room there is a huge sign that I made. It says, "Simplify." It is a constant reminder for me. Every morning I wake up and look at that and it reminds me that life isn't as complicated as it seems sometimes.

Q: How about you, Gabriel? What would you say to the people of the world? How can we change our path?

Gabriel: We need to figure out the true meaning of our lives so we can fulfill our purpose. Every person has a different purpose. Our ultimate goal is to create a world like in those stories where everyone is truly happy.

Lindsay: Black, white, or purple; gay or straight; male or female; fast-food employee or Ivy League lawyer, it doesn't matter. What matters is love. Because if we can't learn to love, what's the point?

16

I feel I represent being in truth
and I'm here to be an
example
of
speaking
and
living
that
truth.

—Ahn

The END IS ONLY *the* BEGINNING

Throughout this work we have listened to the words of our next evolution, the Children of Now, or at least a good sampling of them. Our realities may have been stretched (I hope so!) and the possibilities of our remembering who we are and of what we are capable just got a lit brighter. Our children know. They *really do know*.

Why is it that we as adults continue to struggle when the messages are so clear? Are we so caught up in being successful adults that we forget, within our very heart of hearts, we know more, are more? Or that the possibilities are endless and life is an amazing journey? Probably because we don't give ourselves enough credit. Most likely because we don't remember who we are or from where we have come. For that matter we haven't grasped that life doesn't have to be a continual struggle or butting of heads. Life is a gift. It is an endless adventure within which we can choose to change. In fact *we are the change*.

What have we learned from the Children of Now? Perhaps that human beings are not individually omnipotent, and that perhaps we are indeed part of a greater whole. That there are beings beyond our reality who are loving us and nurturing us from within and from afar. In their ancient traditions and with the wisdom of eons, they bring to us teachings of endless knowledge, but beyond that, the wisdom of the ages. Yes, it does exist.

The children know without a doubt who they are. They know why they are here. Did we ever consciously know that? Did we forget, or was that never really a concern for us?

What else have we gleaned from these magnificents, these wonderful beings of our evolution? We have learned that love is truly unconditional. That we are the ones who dilute love into something that is frivolous and disposable. That love is the basis for all existence and that how we live that existence is our choice.

We have learned that God is us and we are God. That gives us unlimited power. The power to create whatever kind of life we want, whatever kind of world in which we want to live. We have learned that God is not religion, but that religion is merely a human-developed framework that was designed to capture the essence of God. Unfortunately, the essence that was captured was perhaps the singular purpose of those involved at the religion's inception. According to the children, the only God is a Loving God.

The Children of Now tell us many versions about what is beyond the reality that we can see and feel, touch, hear, and smell. The fact that so many of our children, and even nowadays many adults, experience other realities does not make them sick or weird, or in need of treatment. What it does mean that the possibilities that are available to humanity are as endless as the worlds that many encounter.

And what about the material of those in other worlds have to teach us? Perhaps if we could look into those golden books that some of the council beings carry we would know it all...my sense is that if we just got our own ways for a little while we would find much greater reality there, patiently waiting for us.

For many of us, these magnificent Guides have taught the true nature of our existence. How all matter is created and of what. How it all works and how we are part of those intricate workings. The question is do we continue to kick and scream through our lives, resisting all that is available to us through other channels, or do we listen beyond the noise and past the quiet to what is available to us? Do we intentionally create our lives or do we choose to become victims of them? Are we who we are meant to be? What kinds of lives are we creating for ourselves and our world?

Knowing that we live far beyond our bodies both now and when we "die" gives an entirely new perspective about what is important in our lives. The little things really don't matter. We are infinite beings who are created of light, and within that light resides everything that ever was, is, or will be. From what the kids tell us, most of us have been here time and again. Must we cycle through time over and over again, or is there a point where we step into our mastery and claim our infinite heritage? These answers and more are up to us. It is all there for the choosing.

How we change the direction of humanity is up to us. I prefer the way the kids state it. More love. More hugging. More light. Mutual honoring and the acknowledgment that we are all part of an integral One.

From our children we have heard that we should not fear our destiny; rather, create it. What a concept! That leaves the notion of the 2012 phenomenon wide open to the creative process. Instead of dreading change, instead of being afraid, if we take the creative reins into our hands and ride unafraid into every moment that we are, perhaps before we know it we will have affected the change we meant to create. The only way to know for sure is to do it.

Most of all, as we consider each other and our differences, the children have brought up a terrific point. Each of us is part of a giant jigsaw puzzle. It isn't complete with even one of us not participating. Let us look at our differences as part of a greater success. Instead of carrying around false needs or fears, let us be light.

In fact, let us be light.

Bless our children, nurture them. Remember that no matter what anyone says in judgment, your children are your children. Don't let anyone tell you what they need. The children already know, and it isn't drugs, it isn't names or perceptions of difference. What they need is a world of love to inherit.

They can show us the way.

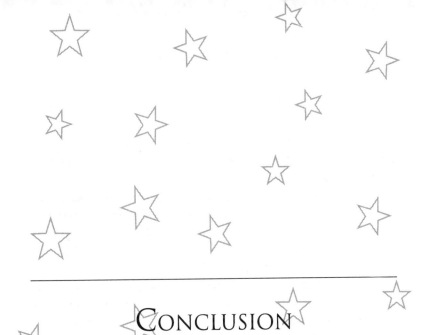

Conclusion

Relaxing in the Knowing of Our Grand Plan
By Nicholas Tschense

There is a plan that is so Grand, it is easy to miss it. As consciousness increases, we no longer even want to ask ourselves, "What is my role in the plan?" as this is a question that evidentiary answers itself.

Through the natural law of Flow, things will arrive at where they are to arrive at whether it is now or later. This is much like the example of water flowing down the River. It can flow in an unobstructed path and arrive sooner. Or it can meet a Rock of resistance that temporarily interrupts its path. Through the natural law of Flow, it flows around with an even greater force to arrive at the same destination.

So you see, natures rhythm and natural laws are taking care of the unfoldment of our Divine Universe now.

What happens from now till 2012 and beyond is a natural cause of our natural laws.

The Rock of Resistance is what we find when we tamper outside of our Natural Laws. Yet like the River, it too shall find its Path.

We are like the River, each of us finding and weaving our own Path, seemingly directing our own flow. Yet, just like a drop of water belongs to the matrix of water, we belong to an almost predestined, preordained matrix of life. The difference here is, as Partners in Life Matrices, we are at a threshold of our evolutionary creation. While it may seem this opportunity asks a lot of us, even this is part of the Divine Plan. This Master Mind of Creation has not left out one nanostrand of subatomic information to complete our Evolutionary Path.

We are being given not only the complete evolutionary data, yet also the complete evolutionary genetic blueprint to arrive at our Grand Celebration.

Poem/song dedicated to my mom and all children leading the way!

OUR GRAND CELEBRATION
THROUGH COCREATION

We are all here in this grand benediction

Yet we need to know to love without affliction.

Crystal Children are here as a new generation

We like to bring love to this whole situation.

So when you ask us what's up for 2012?

The simple answer is a grand celebration.

Coming about through our cocreation.

It is in these times the Crystal Children are arriving in increasing numbers to become an intricate part of the etheric and genetic blueprint. Honoring their presence helps this whole process.

My main message is we can all Relax in the Knowing that our all Loving Masterful Mind has not omitted one detail.

We can relax in the knowing that love is here to stay!

Bringer of Light and Love,

© 2007, Nicholas Tschense, 10 yrs.

www.friendsofnicholas.com

The views and opinions expressed by Nicholas at 10 years of age, may evolve as he matures. The words written were created by use of his letterboard. The term "God" is used as a metaphor to describe Our Creator or whatever term you apply. These messages are meant for all to hear without the exclusion of any one party. These children invite you to listen and respond with your feedback through survey and discussion forum.

Resources

The following are lists of Websites, books, and films that typically have a great deal of information about the Children of Now. These are not recommendations, as the author has not read or experienced every item. Most are recommended to the author by parents, teachers, and other professionals who work with the Children of Now. These are offered as optional tools for learning about the children. As with all other information, please use your discretion...if the information fits, great!

Indigo

www.indigochild.com/

www.artakiane.com/home.htm

www.greatdreams.com/indigo.htm

www.indigochild.net/a_homeframe.htm

www.childrenofthenewearth.com

http://indigochildren.meetup.com/

www.experiencefestival.com/indigo_children

www.starchild.co.za/articles.html

Crystalline

www.spiritlite.com

www.childrenofthenewearth.com

www.friendsofnicholas.com

www.thecrystalchildren.com/

www.metagifted.org/topics/metagifted/crystalChildren/

www.experiencefestival.com/Crystal_Children

www.enchantedlearning.com/Home.html

www.learnnc.org/index.nsf/

www.ket.org/cgi-plex/watch/series.pl?&id=AJONO

www.learner.org/jnorth/current.html

www.learner.org/jnorth/

www.theindigoevolution.com/

www.cosmikids.org

www.childrenlights.com

www.planetlightworker.com

Further Reading

The Children of Now Crystalline Children, Indigo Children, Star Kids, Angels on Earth and the Phenomenon of Transitional Children
   by Dr. Meg Blackburn Losey, Ph.D.

Attention-Deficit Disorder: Natural Alternatives to Drug Therapy (Natural Health Guide)
   by Nancy L. Morse

A.D.D. the Natural Approach
   by Nina Anderson and Howard Peiper

Without Ritalin: A Natural Approach to ADD
   by Samuel A. Berne

Natural Treatments for ADD and Hyperactivity
   by Skye Weintraub

Bach Flower Remedies for Children: A Parents' Guide
   by Barbara Mazzarella

The Essential Flower Essence Handbook
   by Lila Devi

Beyond the Indigo Children: The New Children and the Coming of the Fifth World
   by P.M.H. Atwater

Indigo Children
   by Lee Carroll and Jan Tober

Indigo Celebration
   by Lee Carroll

Creative Activities for Young Children
   by Mary Mayesky

The Secret Spiritual World of Children
    by Tobin Hart, Ph.D.

Raising Your Spirited Child—A Guide for Parents Whose Child Is More Intense, Sensitive, Perceptive, Persistent, and Energetic
    by Mary Sheedy Kurcinka

The Journey Home Children's Edition The Story of Michael Thomas and the Seven Angels
    by Theresa Corley

Upside-Down Brilliance: The Visual Spatial Learner
    by Linda Kreger Silverman, Ph.D.

Spiritually Healing the Indigo Children: The Practical Guide Hand-Book
    by Wayne Dosick, Ph.D. Ellen Kaufman Dosick, MSW.

Ending School Violence Solutions from America's Youth
    by Jason R. Dorsey

Beyond What You See For Teens
    by Nicolette Désirée Groeneveld

Anger and the Indigo Child Transforming Anger into Love
    by Dianne Lancaster

The A.D.D. and A.D.H.D. Diet!
    by Rachel Bell and Dr. Howard Peiper

Seven Secrets to Raising a Happy and Healthy Child
    by Joyce Golden Seyburn Published by Hay House

Born on a Blue Day: Inside the Extraordinary Mind of an Autistic Savant
    by Daniel Tammet

Kids Books

Full Moon Stories: Thirteen Native American Legends
   by Eagle Walking Turtle

Arrow to the Sun—A Pueblo Indian Tale
   by Gerald McDermott

Places of Power
   by Michael DeMunn

Native Plant Stories
   by Joseph Bruchac

The Sacred Tree
   by Four Worlds Development Project

The Little Soul and the Sun
   by Neale Donald Walsh

SunDancer
   by Edward Hays

Hope for the Flowers
   by Trina Paulus

Special Gifts—In Search of Love and Honor
   by Dennis L. Olson

The Children's Book of Virtues
   by William J Bennett

Children of The Sun—A Spiritual Journey Using Story and Songs (includes CD)
   by Laurel Savoie and Emery Bear

People and Places You Can Contact

Meg Blackburn Losey, PhD
www.spiritlite.com or e-mail drmeg@spiritlite.com

The Montessori Schools
www.amshq.org

The Waldorf Schools
www.awsna.org/ or
www.ch.steiner.school.nz/directories/frames/
nzrss.html

The HeartMath System
www.heartmath.com

CH.A.D.D. (Children with Attention Deficit Disorder)
www.chadd.org

Nutri-Chem
www.nutrichem.com

Cell Tech
www.celltech.com This is the Website of Cell Tech, the
organization that sells Klamath Lake blue-green algae.

Magnetic Therapy
www.primapublishing.com
Website of the publisher of the book *Magnetic*
Therapy, by Ron Lawrence, M.D.

Behavioral Physiology Institutes
www.bp.edu

Films

The Indigo Evolution
    by James Twyman, Stephen Simon, Kent Romney and
    Doreen Virtue

Other Valuable Links

www.cem.msu.edu/~cem181h/projects/97/mercury/
#anchor233568

http://academy.d20.co.edu/kadets/lundberg/dna.html

http://articles.news.aol.com/news/
article.adp?id=20051013135209990001 DNA nutrition

www.drboylan.com

www.spiritlite.com

INDEX

ABOUT THE AUTHOR

Meg Blackburn Losey, Ph.D., is the author of *The Children of Now: Crystalline Children, Indigo Children, Star Kids, Angels on Earth, and the Phenomenon of Transitional Children, Pyramids of Light: Awakening to Multi-Dimensional Reality*, and *Online Messages*. Dr. Meg is the hostess of the hit Internet radio show "Continuum," which is broadcast on shirleymaclaine.com. She is a regular columnist in *Mystic Pop Magazine*, a contributor to many other publications, and she is a keynote speaker. Dr. Meg has recently served as a consultant to *Good Morning America*. She can be reached by e-mail at drmeg@spiritlite.com, or on her Website at *www.spiritlite.com*.